# StorySelling

## How to Use the Power of Stories to Lead & Influence Others

By Matthew Linklater

# General Information



**Publisher: Linklater Group, 2021 Midwest Road, Oak Brook, Illinois 60542, United States**

While they have made every effort to verify the information here, neither the author nor the publisher assumes any responsibility for errors in, omissions from or different interpretation of the subject matter. This information may be subject to varying laws and practices in different areas, states and countries. The reader assumes all responsibility for use of the information.

The author and publisher shall in no event be held liable to any party for any damages arising directly or indirectly from any use of this material. Every effort has been made to accurately represent this product and its potential and there is no guarantee that you will earn any money using these techniques.

# Contents

# The Power of StorySelling

LET ME ASK YOU SOMETHING...

Did Martin Luther King have a speech that was a 10-point plan or was it "I have a dream"?

The answer, I think, is obvious.

We are still talking about him today because he was able to inspire people with his dream.

He was able to touch people's hearts and not just their minds and so his message got through.

Or, to put it another way, he was able to tap into their emotions rather than try to convince them with logic.

That's an important lesson that we'll talk about more in a moment.

But first...

## You Could Be Losing Out

Let me ask you something else...

Are you losing out in life because you're failing to get your message across when it matters?

Are you:

- Missing out on sales because you're not connecting with your prospects?
- Being held back in your career because you're not making an impact?
- Losing out because you come off second best in negotiations, whether it's signing a major contract at work or buying a new car?
- Failing to connect with your audiences through presentations that are weak and uninteresting?
- Struggling to get your message across in your writing?
- Going the wrong direction in your social life because you usually end up doing what others want?
- Frustrated every time you have to get on the phone to customer services for any service you pay for?

If you recognize any of these situations, the most likely problem is that you are failing to get your message across.

So imagine instead that you could move an audience the way MLK did – whether you're chatting to your partner, trying to persuade a prospect or addressing an audience of thousands.

Now I'm not saying you're going to make history – though perhaps you will.

I am suggesting, however, that there are skills and secrets that are known to highly successful communicators that maybe you haven't yet mastered.

## The Power of Unconscious Communication

**The key to communicating what you want is connecting with the limbic brain.**

Let me share a bit of the science behind this. Usually when we make a decision, it is based on an emotional response and then afterwards, we justify it by logic.

You can think of the times that you've made decisions – perhaps especially with bad decisions.

You reflect on them, you know they're emotional decisions and then later, you justify them by logic.

This happens because we have two parts of our brain involved in making decisions – the Limbic Brain and Neocortex.

- The **Limbic Brain** is the reptilian brain. It does not understand logic. It only understands stories, pictures and symbols and this is the brain that makes us respond.
- The **Neocortex** is the one that we use logic to understand stuff.

The key to communicating what you want is connecting with the limbic brain.

That's what MLK did in his famous, passionate speech.

But most people make the mistake of focusing on facts and details in their communication and therefore go directly to the neocortex without engaging the limbic brain.

The secrets I'll share in this book are about how you can engage the limbic brain first and get the result you want.

## How It Could Be

Imagine instead that you could confidently and easily communicate with others to convince them of your point of view.

You'd soon start:

- Making sales more easily
- Coming out top in negotiations
- Delivering presentations that are interesting and effective
- Writing in a way that others want to read
- Taking charge of your social life
- Winning the battle with customer service departments

In this book, I'm going to share with you some powerful secrets that can transform your ability to communicate with others.

I'm also going to show you how you can change the way you communicate with yourself so you can change your own behavior and how you think.

As a result, you'll see a major change for the better in all areas of your life.

These skills are particularly important if you work in an area such as sales or negotiation where it's important to encourage others to your point of view.

But it's a skill that applies widely.

## Why These Skills Matter

I've called the book StorySelling because it revolves around using the power of stories to get your message across.

But I'll be sharing skills that apply to virtually everyone.

I know you may not think of yourself as a salesperson.

But the truth is that every day, you're selling somebody.

- You're selling your kids on why to get better grades.
- You're selling your husband to stop putting his underwear on the floor.
- You're selling your wife on why you'll be watching the big game rather than going shopping.
- If you're in leadership, you're selling the people that you lead on setting a higher standard for themselves.
- You're selling that person who's maybe not working as hard at work just to put a little bit extra effort in each and every day.

The truth is we're all salespeople in some way.

When it comes down to sales skills, Stanford Research Institute did very important study, which said the following:

The money you make in any endeavor is determined only 12.5% by knowledge and 87.5% by your ability to deal with people.

A very simple formula that I put together is this.

Your success in closing any sale is:

**87.5% your soft skills**

**+ 12.5% your product knowledge**

**= Your ability to close sales**

See knowledge on products – or virtually any topic – is easy to come by.

Anybody can memorize a fact card. Anybody could read information and become very knowledgeable about something.

But the reality is, how many people can communicate that information in such a way that they make an impact?

One of the keys to doing that is knowing how to make use of stories in your communication.

With what you learn in this book, you'll become one of those people who know how to make an impact.

**The money you make in any endeavor is determined only 12.5% by knowledge.**

## In This Book

The book shares the information in 10 core segments.

1. Why You Should Use Stories to Communicate
2. The Science Behind Why Stories Work
3. The Difference Stories Can Make
4. How to Control Communication Through Specificity
5. Four Keys to Communication That Works
6. Using 3-D Communication to Get the Message Across
7. How to Construct a Powerful Story or Metaphor
8. Using Reframing to Change Minds
9. Six Secrets of Influence That Will Transform Your Messages
10. Creating Your Own Dream Story

Finally, once we've talked about how to use stories, I'll share some effective metaphors that you can model to help get your own message across.

So we'll finish up with my Million Dollar Metaphor Library.

I promise you that my techniques, and this book, are full of value, but you're getting them at a reduced price compared to the rewards.

A little time and a little practice will pay off in huge dividends.

This promise goes for any walk of professional life – and I extend this promise to your personal agendas as well.

Please enjoy! I know you will.

**Matthew Linklater**

# Chapter 1

## Why You Should Use Stories to Communicate

I WANT TO SHARE WITH YOU JUST A VERY QUICK STORY.

Jack Nicklaus is arguably the greatest golfer of all time. They call him the Golden Bear.

The story is Jack was asked by the king of Saudi Arabia to come and play golf. Jack said, "You know, I'm okay. I don't want to come play."

The king was really persistent and the king said, "I'll tell you what. I'll send over my private jet to come pick you up, fly you over here, and we'll have a great week."

So Jack said, "All right, if you're going to send your private jet, I'll come on over and play."

He goes over and plays golf with the king for the week. At the end of the week, the king says, "Jack, you came and played golf with me. This was the greatest week of my life. What can I do for you?"

Jack, again, modestly said, "You know, I'm okay. I had the greatest week of my life. I ate like a king. I drank like a king. I played on some of the greatest golf courses in the world, so I'm okay."

**Stories and metaphors are hugely impactful in persuasion.**

The king was really persistent, so Jack finally said, "I'll tell you what. I collect golf clubs. Buy me a golf club." The king said, "Consider it done."

Jack's on the way back to the United States on the king's private jet. You can imagine this thing's gaudier than anything Donald Trump could dream up. It's gold-plated, it's jewel-encrusted, it's diamond-encrusted.

Jack's imagination's running wild. "What kind of golf club am I going to get?" He's imagined a gold-plated golf club with his name etched on it. He's imagined a jewel-encrusted golf club, a diamond-encrusted golf club. His imagination is just going wild all the way home.

He gets back to the United States and he's carrying on with his normal, daily activities. He really does collect golf clubs, so his imagination is going.

After about 90 days, he hears nothing from the king and, shortly thereafter, he gets a letter in the mail from the king of Saudi Arabia.

He said, "This is weird. I asked for a golf club."

Jack opens up the letter and in the letter is a deed for a 500-acre golf club.

You see, the king thinks quite a bit bigger than Jack.

Now you might wonder what that story has to do with you and your business or your life.

Well this book is all about how to harness the power of stories and metaphors in your business and in your life.

## The Impact of Stories

Stories and metaphors are hugely impactful in persuasion.

Here are just a few of the ways you can use them to transform your results.

- **Overcoming objections.** Having a great story to overcome an objection will increase and enhance your persuasion.
- **Install a Belief.** You can use a story to install a belief into somebody and it helps the other person to be able to listen uncritically.

  As I said earlier, we can understand large amounts of facts, figures, and data logically with our neocortex brain. But our limbic brain only understands metaphors and stories and symbols.

  If we can hit that, we can help people listen uncritically.

- **Connect emotionally to our audience.** How we connect emotionally is through a story.

  The story evokes emotion, typically, and the story draws people into you to help create that emotional connection and that rapport.

- **Keys to persuasion.** Lastly, I believe stories and metaphors are the keys to persuasion.

In the rest of this book, I'm going to show how to dive deeper into this to really understand what stories and metaphors are, and how to use them so you can be more impactful with your communication.

# Chapter 2

## The Science Behind Why Stories Work

IN THIS SEGMENT, I WANT TO SHARE WITH YOU WHY STORIES ARE SO IMPORTANT TO YOUR COMMUNICATION.

I'll show you what a story actually accomplishes with you, with your audience, and with your persuasiveness.

In the introduction, I talked about the difference between the limbic brain and the neocortex brain.

The limbic brain is the oldest brain and the neocortex brain is the newest brain for humans.

You've probably heard for example that sales are made based on emotion and buyers justify them by logic.

So a key to making more sales is hitting the emotion before you bring in the logic.

Many of us in our communication tend to go first to the logic. We want to bring in the facts, the figures, the numbers.

**If you can connect with somebody emotionally, you're going to have more success with getting your message across.**

But the reality is if you can connect with somebody emotionally and hit their limbic brain, you're going to have more success with getting your message across.

You're going to have more success installing a new belief in that person, which is more consistent with the message you want to get across.

**A key to making more sales is hitting the emotion before you bring in the logic.**

Let's say someone is not taking the action you want them to take and you want to install a new belief into that person.

The best way to do it is by hitting their limbic brain and hitting that emotional brain.

Once you get that emotional buy-in, you're going to have more success. Here's the key...

- The limbic brain only deals in stories, metaphors, and symbols. It's an emotional part of the brain.
- The neocortex deals in logic and figures and facts.

Certainly we can convince someone by bombarding them with a lot of facts, figures, and logic.

But doing it that way will take a lot longer than if you can hit the limbic and you can hit their emotional part of their brain.

When you start out with a story, you will open up their mind and hit them more emotionally.

## Conscious and Unconscious Communication

**When you start out with a story, you will open up their mind and hit them more emotionally.**

Let's talk about how that happens and why that happens.

This comes down to the difference between the unconscious mind versus the conscious mind.

As you're sitting reading this, what I want you to do is this. I want you to put your hand on the table.

Put your right hand on the table and lift it straight up.

As you do that, I want to ask you a question.

Was that a conscious movement or unconscious movement?

Unequivocally, in all my seminars, people say that was done consciously.

Well, certainly you did it with conscious volition, but unconsciously there are 134 muscles between your arm and your hand that move your arm.

So you had to do it unconsciously.

Here's another thing...

How many degrees is a right angle?

Well, 90 degrees. When was the last time you thought about that? Probably not since high school.

I'm here to tell you that all learning, all change, and all your beliefs are stored unconsciously.

If all your learning is done unconsciously, all your beliefs are stored unconsciously:

- How do you change somebody's beliefs?
- How do you get them to see something a new way?
- How do you get them to change their behavior?

You know that it's hard to change a bad habit. It's hard to change a belief.

If you're a smoker, it's hard to change that habit.

That's with all our beliefs and that's with all that we believe we know.

The only way that you're going to get somebody to change is by tapping into their unconscious mind and a story does that.

Let me explain exactly how a story does that.

Let's say here's your mind:

- At the bottom, you have your **Conscious Mind.**
- At the top, you have your **Unconscious Mind.**
- In the middle, you have what's called your **Critical Faculty Barrier.**

What happens is when you take in new information, you say this is true or this is false and you say yes or you say no.

When information comes in, you either allow it in or you stop it from coming in.

If you allow it in, you take it on and play out a new belief.

For example, if you're watching TV nowadays...

My mom, for instance, watches a lot of news. I live in downtown Chicago and, talking to my mom, you would think I live in the middle of a war zone.

Because they talk about all the gang fights and everything out there, that's her belief. When she comes downtown, she's actually a little bit nervous.

She lets that story come in uncritically and then she plays it out.

Not to pick on my mom here, but let me tell you another story. She was 60 years old and she needed to find a new job.

She said, "Matt, I'm going to go look at Walmart." I said, "Okay, that's a great idea. Ride that wave until you're 66."

But she goes, "They don't want to hire somebody who's 60 years old."

I looked at her. "Mom, who do you think works at Walmart? They're all 60 years old. They're all older than 60."

**The only way you're going to get somebody to change is by tapping into their unconscious mind and a story does that.**

But my mom had the belief that they weren't going to hire her.

She went in there and filled out an application and she left off her age. She didn't get a call back.

I ask this question. What is the weeding out process at Walmart?

How many applications do you think they get a day? Hundreds, maybe a thousand?

The weeding out process, is it age or an incomplete application? It's an incomplete application.

Now what did my mom say? It was age.

So we have these strong beliefs through our unconscious mind.

## What Stories Do

What a story does is allows you to plant a belief into somebody's mind (or in your own mind).

Let me explain to you.

### Suspending Disbelief

You have to suspend your disbelief.

When you suspend your disbelief, you take on a new learning, a new idea, a new belief, and you go out and play it out.

If you're watching TV, say, since 2008, we have had high unemployment, the economy this, the economy that.

If you believe that, you go out there and you play that out.

> **What a story does is allows you to plant a belief into somebody's mind.**

I say this. During the Great Depression, there was 30% unemployment, but there was 70% employment.

But people take on that belief and that story because they hear it through the stories in the news.

It causes a trance.

### Trancing Out

Do you ever see when people are watching the TV and you're saying, "Hey, Matt. Hey, Matt!"

You're trying to get their attention and they're just tranced out on the TV because the TV is telling a story and bypassing their critical faculty barrier and putting them in what's called a light trance.

I'm sure you've had that happen before where somebody's watching and you just can't get through to them.

Ultimately that's what a story does. It puts their defenses down and puts them into a light trance and allows you to slip in a new idea, a new belief.

I'll share with you how to do all that.

One thing I will caution you is, please do this ethically because you can certainly use some of these persuasive techniques unethically, so we want to make sure that we're using them 100% ethically.

## How to Make It Work

So how do you suspend your disbelief?

Think about it. You've watched a superhero movie. You've watched Iron Man, for instance. As you see Tony Stark, you start believing, "Hey, this could happen. This is pretty cool."

Maybe you even start imagining yourself as Tony Stark or you start fantasizing about it.

The only way that you can even watch that is if you suspend your disbelief because your critical faculties will say, "This isn't true. This is never happening. This can't happen."

But you suspend your disbelief through a story and you start taking on a belief that, "Maybe this is possible," even if it's for a short period of time.

A story and a metaphor helps you suspend your disbelief by bypassing the critical faculty barrier and installs a new belief, a new learning, and it helps change behavior because all that is stored at the unconscious.

**A story and a metaphor helps you suspend your disbelief by bypassing the critical faculty barrier and installs a new belief.**

**How This Works**

Let's talk a little bit more about how all this works. Let's look at where the story and the metaphor fits and then I'll give you some examples.

In the diagram on page 19, you can see that your critical faculty barrier sits in the middle between your unconscious mind and your conscious mind.

When we try to get someone to take on a new belief unconsciously, we have to start with their conscious which is their current belief or problem.

In order to change their belief, you're bumping into the critical faculty barrier trying to explain your product, your solution, your benefit.

Ultimately what you do in the story is provide a way to jump over the critical faculty barrier.

When you have a story and you link their current beliefs and their behaviors to a new belief and a new behavior, that's ultimately what a story's going to do.

It will open up their mind, bypass their critical faculty barrier, and ultimately take them to a new belief.

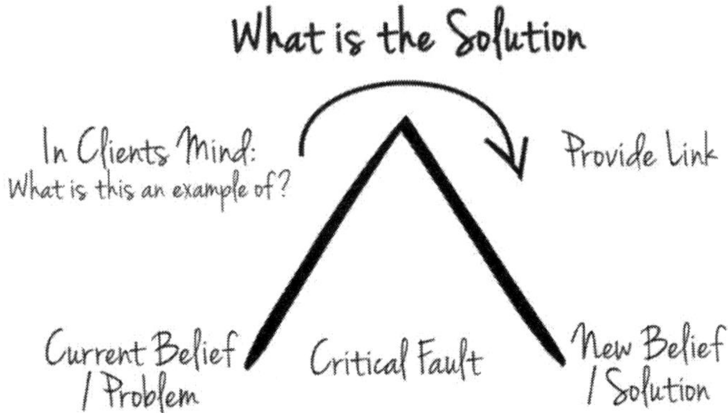


What you have to think about... and I'll be going in to this in more detail later... is you have to think about, in the other person's mind what is this an example of? What is this problem, what is this belief an example of?

Then you construct your story and provide a link to the new belief.

To illustrate it, let me give you two quick stories.

For instance, a client says, "Hey, you're too expensive."

We can use the following Pablo Picasso story.

*Pablo Picasso is sitting in a café. A lady comes up to him and says, "You know, Mr. Picasso, I never thought I was going to meet you. I've always dreamed of you painting my portrait."*

*Pablo Picasso said, "Hey, I'm with my friends." The lady said, "No, I'll pay you for it."*

*Picasso says, "Okay," takes out his sketch pad and sketches it up. Within five minutes he's done.*

*He gives it to the lady. The lady's ecstatic, "Oh my God, Pablo. This is the greatest thing I've ever seen. I have to pay you for this. How much is this?"*

*He looked at her and he said, "It's 10,000 francs."*

*The lady said, "10,000 francs? Are you crazy? That took you five minutes. It's only five minutes of work."*

*Pablo looked at her and said, "Ma'am, I beg to differ with you. This was a lifetime of work that went into that picture for you."*

Really, it's not just about the price that you're paying. It's about all the value and benefits that you're getting behind it.

Another gentleman came into an advisor's office and said, "I don't need your product. I just need your free report. I don't need your solutions. I don't need your plan. I already have a plan."

The advisor said to him:

*"I totally understand where you're coming from. You sold copiers your whole life. I have to ask you a question. Did you ever go into a business owner where maybe it was an older business owner and you know he had a copier in the corner that was costing him money and costing him time and productivity?*

*And he said, 'I don't need a new copier. The one I have is the best.' But you knew that a new copier could save him money and save him time, so you persuaded him to buy a new copier?*

*Then a week later he comes to you and says, 'That copier is the best thing I'd ever bought. I didn't realize I was sitting on such a crappy, old copier and using something so archaic.'"*

*Well, that's the same thing we're doing here. The client had the belief they didn't need anything.*

*Their plan was fine. You paced them through that they had an old, crappy copier in the corner and you paced them through a brand new copier that's going to be more efficient for their plan.*

Ultimately, at the end, when you're thinking of a story and a metaphor and a reframe, it boils down to this.

How do you change the context or change the content of the current belief or the current idea the client has?

We'll look at that in more detail in the chapter on How to Use Reframing to Change Minds.

In short, that's how stories work. That's what stories will do for your business.

Later I'm going to share with you how you construct a great story and how you start utilizing stories in your business and in your life.

But first, let's look at the different ways in which stories can make a difference.

# Chapter 3

## The Difference Stories Can Make

I WANT TO SHARE WITH YOU SOME POSSIBILITIES OF UTILIZING STORIES.

So what are some areas that you could use stories?
**Making Presentations More Powerful**

Ultimately, I think that in presentations, you should use a story as a grabber opener.

There's a lot of things you can do. You can use props with stories. I used to hand out snorkels to everybody and tell about a snorkeling trip that I had and how the waters were rough. I was getting sick.

They told me to look out at the horizon because I'd feel better and it didn't make me feel better.

But ultimately I knew that one day, I was going to be back on that land and on that horizon.

> **You can use stories and metaphors as grabber openings to your presentation.**

I used to tell all types of stories in an opening.

I used to hold up a football and talk about Vince Lombardi and say, "Gentlemen, this is a football and why did Vince Lombardi start his season like that?

Because it's not about learning more esoteric things about football, it's about doing the blocking, tackling, doing the basics well."

You can use stories and metaphors – with or without props – as grabber openings to your presentation.

**Pace and Lead Your Audience**

Stories also allow you to pace and lead through the presentation.

For instance, if you're telling a story, you don't have to just tell the story and end it. You can tell the story and keep going back to the story throughout your presentation.

I use about my grandma a lot during presentations and identifying some of the risks of retirement and the risks of your money.

Granny grew up during the Great Depression. So I'd talk about the stock market and I'd talk about inflation.

Inflation was up about 1000%. I'd talk about withdrawal rates on your money.

I'd talk about longevity. Granny lived to 94.

I'd go through and talk a lot about Granny and her life experiences and how they tied to people's life experiences and the major risks with their money.

You can take that through a whole presentation, whether that be a five-minute presentation, a 20-minute presentation, an hour presentation.

You can start with the story and you keep that story ambiguous all the way through until you close it at the end.

You can close out the story at the end or leave it ambiguous. So you can use the story to help pace and lead your audience.

**Use Open Loops to Maintain Interest**

When you tell a story and you don't end the story, it leaves your listener wanting more.

It creates what's called an open loop. If you use a story and you don't close the end of it, it creates an open loop so that people are asking for more communication.

**When you tell a story and you don't end the story, it leaves your listener wanting more.**

They're looking for the answer. They might not be doing it consciously, but unconsciously.

If you don't finish the story, they're looking for the story's outcome.

They're looking for the success of the story throughout your whole presentation, so it's a communication strategy to keep their mind open throughout your whole presentation.

## Connect Emotionally

Stories allow you to connect emotionally to your clients.

I won't get into this too much here, but I'm a high-visual guy. I speak fast in my presentation style.

We'll talk more about communication styles in the chapter on 3-D Communication.

People who are kinesthetic, don't speak as fast as I, and so typically when you start with a story, you can draw in those kinesthetic folks because they're more feelings oriented.

You can connect emotionally through a story because everybody likes a good story.

Everybody likes a good problem that has a good resolution, so they can connect to the people, to the characters in the story.

So they're going to connect emotionally to that story, especially if you have a story that resonates with your whole audience.

> **You can connect emotionally through a story because everybody likes a good story.**

## Change Beliefs

Next, you can use story to change a belief in your audience.

Everybody has a certain belief. They're doing business a certain way. How do you change that belief?

You want to reframe the way the person is currently thinking to frame up the way you want them to think and the way you do business.

We'll talk more about reframing later.

You can help change that belief through story because a story typically touches on a reframe, so it's framing up the way they currently think and reframing into what you want.

## Bring Down Defenses

> **If you can bypass that critical faculty barrier and hit the unconscious mind, you're going to bring down the defenses.**

Ultimately, the story's going to bring down somebody else's defenses.

If you can bypass that critical faculty barrier and hit the unconscious mind, you're going to bring down the defenses.

Let me share with you how you bring down somebody's defenses.

Have you ever argued with somebody over politics? Now politics is so silly because typically logic is never in the equation with politics.

Someone has this total emotional belief that something should happen and they try to apply logic to it.

If you start bringing data points to somebody, especially about politics, you just hit a brick wall.

People don't care because it's more of an emotional discussion.

If you tell a story, what's going to happen is you're going to bypass that logic or that illogic that people sometimes use, whether it be talking about politics or anything.

Sometimes people have an illogical idea that's defending their belief. Their logic just does not make sense.

If you go at them with logic, you're not going to bring down their defenses.

Ultimately, you want to tell a story or an idea or an example that will bypass that critical faculty, bring down their defenses, and install a new belief or at least show them a new way to reframe the way they're currently thinking.

# Chapter 4

## How to Control Communication Through Specificity

NOW I WANT TO SHARE WITH YOU SOME STRATEGIES FOR MAKING YOUR STORIES BETTER.

We've talked about the importance of stories and metaphors and the difference they can make to your communication and persuasion skills.

But the better you make your stories, the better the results.

In the next few chapters, I'm going to show you ways to make your stories better.

The first concept I want to cover is one that assists us in our ability to move through and between different levels of abstraction, from vague and ambiguous to concrete and specific.

**The path to true success involves the ability see the big picture.**

It's sometimes called "chunking" and its full title is the Ladder of Abstraction & Specificity.

This skill is directly related to your ability to move up the corporate ladder, manage people effectively and consistently win sales and negotiations.

Most people bury their heads within the details and get bogged down in the weeds, but the path to true success involves the ability see the big picture.

Sometimes the forest seems vast and never ending when you are among the trees, but if you pull up and hover above the forest you realize the tree line does end.

You also realize that there are many other forests out there to conquer.

The Ladder of Abstraction & Specificity also utilizes the concept of chunks of information.

We have an ability to take an information chunk and:

- Chunk up to a higher level of abstraction
- Chunk down to a lower level of specificity
- Chunk sideways, or laterally at the same level of abstraction

To break it down further:

**The person who controls the level of abstraction within the communication controls the communication itself.**

- When we chunk up we become more general or abstract
- When we chunk down we become more specific
- When we chunk across we stay at the same level of generality

In interpersonal communication the person who controls the level of abstraction within the communication controls the communication itself. I know and you know that this strategy works in all walks of life.

Can you imagine where you can use this?

Let me illustrate how this works with the simple example of a watch. You will see how easily this can be done. Together, we will chunk up, chunk down and chunk laterally.

## Chunking Down

If we chunk down on "watch," we move to a lower level of abstraction, or something more concrete and specific.

We can chunk down and gain specificity by asking for examples. If the subject of the communication was a watch, we might ask:

- What type of watch specifically?
  After getting an answer, we can chunk down to Rolex or Cartier, for example.

If we require further detail – and we often do – we could chunk down one more level by asking:

- What model of Cartier?
  We might get a response of the Roadster or Tank.

In this particular example, we've chunked down on the class or category of the subject in question.

An alternative method of gaining specificity is to chunk down on parts.

For example, instead of chunking down from watch to maker to model, we chunk down from watch to essential watch parts or to the material used for the watch bracelet.

With each increasing level of specificity, we are moving down through the hierarchy of ideas, down through levels of abstraction.

We can gain specificity in interpersonal communication by chunking down, uncovering increasingly fine levels of detail through asking the questions:

- What are examples of this?
- What specifically?

Detail and specificity are useful in particular circumstances and for certain applications.

## Chunking Up

At the other end of the spectrum, there are circumstances and applications that are better served by taking an overall "big picture" view.

When we've been bogged down in the details and we want to look at the big picture, or if we'd simply rather take a 30,000-foot view of things, we chunk up. We need this view once in a while, don't we?

Questions that we can ask to assist us in chunking up include:

- What is this an example of?
- For what purpose?
- What is your intention?

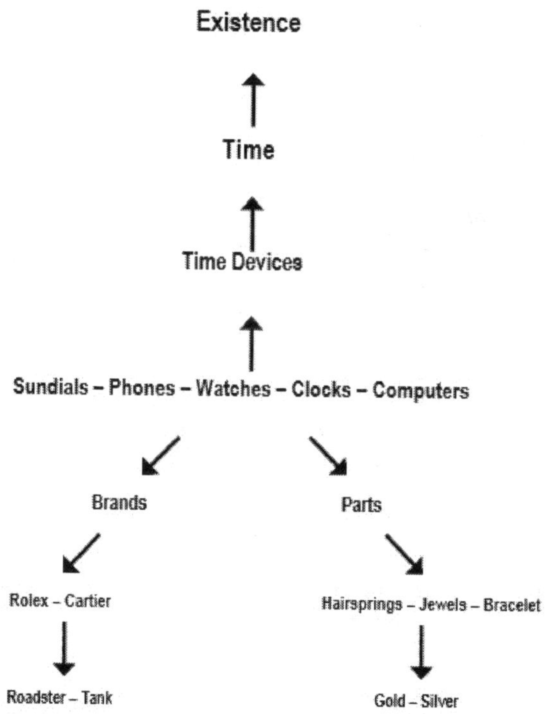

Let's return to our previous example of the watch. If we want to chunk up one level, we can ask the question, "What is this an example of?"

We may chunk up to the subject of time devices.

If we chunk up one more level by asking the question again, we may chunk up to the concept of time in general.

Chunk up again and we may arrive eventually at our existence.

With every level we chunk up, we move to a higher level of abstraction. I'm sure you agree that existence is a far more abstract concept than a watch, don't you?

You can significantly enhance both your cognitive and communication skills by developing your ability to utilize chunking more effectively.

The best salespeople and managers agree. I also believe most successful people know this is an easy - and effective - technique.

If you prefer plain speaking, another way to say it is that being able to chunk effectively will help you to think and communicate better. Who doesn't want that?

## Chunking Sideways

Thus far, we've looked at chunking down to fine details and chunking up to the big picture.

In the same way you will benefit from being able to chunk up and down skillfully, you will benefit even more from being able to chunk laterally, or sideways.

The world's most intuitive problem solvers are masterfully skilled at chunking sideways, and this is a great class of people to be associated with. We would all like to be better problem solvers on the spot, right?

**You can significantly enhance your communication skills by developing your ability to utilize chunking more effectively.**

How do we chunk sideways? It's easy.

- First, chunk up one level.
- Next, chunk down somewhere else.

For example, if we take the word "painting" and chunk up one level, we could chunk up to art. We can ask ourselves, "What are other examples of art?" We could chunk down to sculpture, music, dance or any number of art forms.

By using this simple process of chunking up and then back down, we've effectively chunked sideways. In this particular context, we chunked up from painting to art, then sideways and down again to sculpture, music and dance.

To break it down further, when we chunk sideways we begin by chunking up to one hierarchical level and end by chunking back down to the beginning hierarchical level. Thus, the chunks we end with are on the same level as the chunk where we started.

## Using Your Chunking Skills to Improve Communication

Communication flows better and is more useful when all of the people involved are using similar-sized chunks from the same hierarchical level.

This is also a key reason why the person controlling the level of abstraction also controls the communication.

This will allow you to be more powerful and effective with your communication.

Particularly good uses of lateral chunking involve negotiating, sales, problem solving, humor (think about the comparisons comedians make) and other areas in which you need to successfully communicate.

For example, I saw Carrot Top in Las Vegas recently, and his props are the result of lateral chunks, as illustrated in this diagram.

When you become skilled at chunking up, down and sideways, you will notice an exponential increase in your communication skills and a commanded respect in interpersonal conversations.

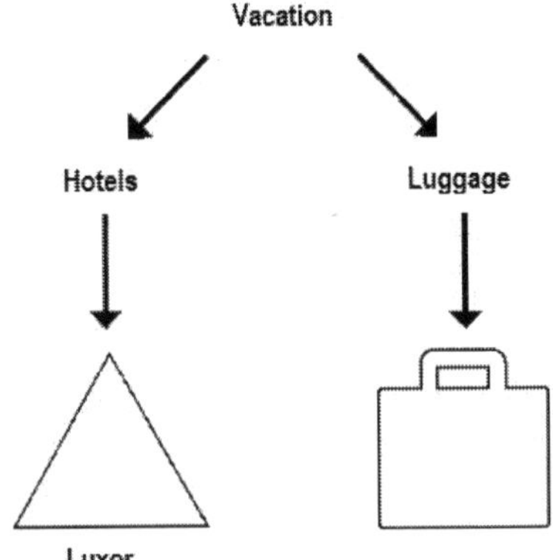

You will notice a growing ability to think circles around your fellow communicators.

How would this benefit you? The possibilities are endless.

Chunking is a great example of being nestled closely among the trees while being able to move up and abstractly see the forest.

Chunking up is essential in persuasion and in selling, well, actually in anything.

For example, when a client is focused on the details of the sale, such as the price, there is only one way to achieve success. Chunk up!

It's necessary to identify with the details, or chunk down, but knowing how to chunk up and frame the big picture adds to the value and justifies the price.

- Sales Professional – Ultimate Goal – Forest
- Client – Price - Trees

In this chart, I've broken it down into a picture for you visual learners.

Your ability to freely chunk up, down and sideways is directly related to your problem solving ability.

People who can see all angles of a circumstance, an event or a problem can more easily discover different pathways to success. Would you like more options in your life?

Understanding chunking is vital for creating effective metaphors.

(More Abstract)

**Agreement**

**What is this an example of?**

**For what purpose?**

**What is your intention?**

**What are other examples of this?**

**What specifically...?**

(More Specific)

**Details**

# Chapter 5

## Four Keys to Communication That Works

THERE'S A VERY POWERFUL FORMULA GIVING THE FOUR KEY ELEMENTS OF EFFECTIVE COMMUNICATION.

It reflects our four learning styles and is called the 4-MAT system. It's how I design all my presentations and writing.

I give you a story, the why, draw you in, tell you what we're learning and tell you how to do it.

Then, if I'm doing a training, people go and do it and then they have some questions back to me. We follow that format in everything I do.

David Kolb came up with these and a lady named Bernice McCarthy put them together in the way that I use them.

The four learning styles reflect the fact that people want to know:

- Why?
- What?
- How?
- What if?

This concept is rooted in science – biology as well as psychology!

As I mentioned in the introduction, we have a couple of layers of brain if you will, and one is our neocortex.

Our neocortex deals in logic, it deals in vast numbers of facts, figures, numbers.

But then we also have the limbic brain, and the limbic brain doesn't deal in facts, figures, logic.

- It deals in emotions.
- It deals in pictures.
- It deals in symbols.
- It deals in archetypes.
- It deals in feelings.

It is the part of the brain that is responsible for the chemical reactions.

Before your neocortex can even comprehend logically what's happening, your limbic brain has already made a decision.

So how do you tap into people's limbic brains? How do you tap into that part of the brain that is emotionally based, that acts in an instant, and then later comes a justification of logic?

You have to start with hitting that limbic brain and starting with why.

## Starting with Why

Let me share with you a couple of stories of how I utilize starting with why.

For instance, my wife was moving from San Francisco to Chicago.

She enjoys going to the spa, she likes spa services and when she moved here she said, "You know, none of the spas in Chicago are even comparable to the spas in California."

After trying out a few different spas, she found one that she really liked and settled on it.

I'd just learned this new strategy so I was like, "Hey, let me go in there and get her a gift certificate for her birthday that's coming up."

I went in there and I said, "You know what? My wife really loves this place. She moved here from California. She says no spas in Chicago even compare to the spas in California. Now she tells all her friends and everybody she meets about this place. That's how much she's in love with it, and I want to get her a gift certificate for her birthday. I want to get her a $200 gift certificate. Do you mind putting twenty percent on top? She would love it. She would tell everybody."

What do you think they said? They said, "Sure, that would be no problem."

If I would have gone in and told them <u>what</u> I want, "I want to buy a $200 gift certificate, can you put twenty percent on top?" they would have looked at me like I was crazy or I had a third eye.

The problem is a lot of times when we go in to a situation, we go in with what we have or what we want, rather than the reasons of why it's important in front.

Another example was in Robert Cialdini's book, "Influence."

He talks about a lady who was cutting in line at a library to make some copies. She went up the line and said, "I need to make ten copies, can I cut?"

**The problem is a lot of times, we go in to a situation with what we want, rather than the reasons why it's important in front.**

67% of the time people actually let her cut, by just saying I need to make ten copies.

However, when she put a reason why she needed to cut in line in front of that she needed to make ten copies, her compliance went up to over 93% that people let her cut.

By simply saying, "I'm late to pick up my kids at soccer practice, I need to make ten copies, do you mind if I cut in line?" her compliance went from 67% to over 93%.

Giving them a reason why made a huge difference.

Here's another example. I recently was selling some houses in Michigan and the Western Michigan University was who I was selling them to. They kept low balling me.

My realtor said, "You know, Matt, you should come down in price."

I said, "Let me sleep on it." I slept on it and I came back with this story. But I had to teach my realtor how to tell this story because he had to put the reasons why I was going to stay at full price in front of saying that we're staying at full price.

> **If you can put the reasons why in front of your communication, you're going to have more success.**

Here's what he said to the school, "Look, in this transaction, you want to have these houses completely empty in ninety days. You want a ninety day close. If this close does not go through, my client stands, one, to lose a lot a money, but two, to have a bunch of empty houses, so that will compound on itself. My client needs to stay at full price."

The lawyer on the other side said, "Oh wow, we didn't know that. That's not a problem."

What I'm saying is, if you can put the reasons why in front of your communication, you're going to have more success.

## Four Learning Styles

Now let's look at the four learning styles in a bit more detail.

**Why?**

Why people want to know why and why not. They want to know why something is worth doing. They want to explore the reasons for taking action before doing so.

This group is 35% of people.

They study life as it is and reflect on it. They seek meaning. They need reasons and relevance.

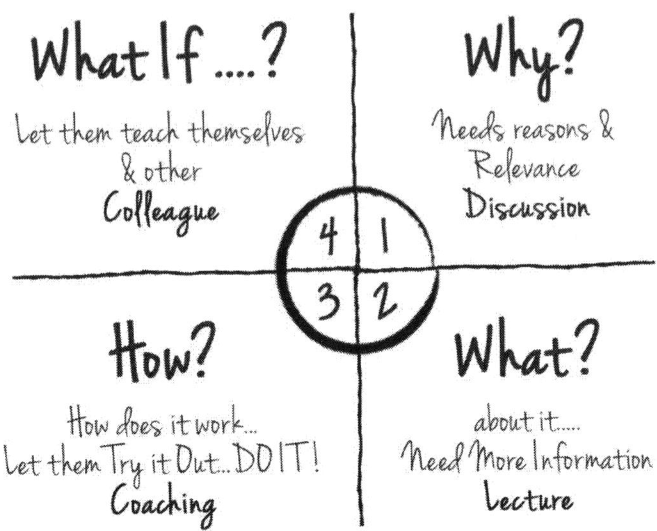


They learn best by listening and sharing ideas with others. They like discussion.

**What?**

The next element is the what. This group of people wants more information. They need to know the what.

This part of your communication is where you disseminate information. These people like to have lots of information whether delivered orally or in printed documents.

They learn best by thinking through ideas. They like to analyze. As students they love to take lots of notes.

These are 22% of the people.

What you want to talk about here is everything that supports your message.

What data or research, what third party, what economy, what is going on in the economy that helps frame the way the person takes on board your message.

**How?**

The next category is how. How does it work? Let them try it out. Let them do it. They need exercises.

You can tell them the secrets of how it works. This person starts with an idea, tries it out, testing to see if it works, seeks usability, and needs to know how things work.

They learn best by testing theories in ways that make sense, teaching with common sense, coaching and facilitating.

This group is 18% of the people.

**What If?**

The fourth category is the what if people. This makes up 25% of the people.

The way they learn is to let them teach themselves and others. They learn through trial and error.

These are folks who when we're done with an exercise, they like to ask questions and reflect on it.

These peoples seek hidden possibilities and needs to know what can be done with something.

Lastly it's about what if I'm interested, what's next? What are the next steps?

All of these need to come in the specific order:

1. Why?
2. What?
3. Who?
4. What if?

People need to know the why before the what, before the how, before the what if.

- The "Why?" people won't wait till the end
- The "What?" people will wait for the why
- The "How?" people will wait for the why and the what
- The "What if?" people will wait for the how, what, and why

## Building a Strong Why

Here are some tips on how to build a strong why and structure your message effectively.

**1. Reasons**

Number one, you want to start with reasons. What are the reasons why someone should listen to you? What are the reasons why what you have to say is important?

**2. X-factor**

When you look at your product or service, what is the x-factor?

What I mean by that is 80% of all products or services are about the same, it's the 20% that make the difference.

That 20% has the x-factor, so what is the x-factor of your product or service?

### 3. "Yes Set"

Another thing you can do is utilize a yes set. Three undeniable truths or three questions that the person is going to say yes to.

Here's a simple example:

*"Mr. and Mrs. Client, do you have some money that's sitting on the sidelines?" Yes.*

*"Are people being more conservative with their investments over the last five or six years?" Yes.*

*"Are clients really concerned about their portfolios and what that would mean for their retirement?" Yes.*

*"Great, let me share with you exactly what we do to mitigate those three things and secure their retirement."*

So you could start with a yes set.

### 4. Universal Quantifier

Another option is a universal quantifier. These are three undeniable true statements, that the majority of people would say yes to.

What could you say that the majority of the people would say yes to, or agree with? You can use those as statements.

### 5. Highlight Keys

Then here's another way to build your why.

What we recommend is that you have three to five bullet points in your 'what' section and three to five bullet points in your 'how' section of your presentation.

When you look at what supports 'how' in a financial presentation, you might have three to five bullet points of what you're going to talk about, maybe third party research, things in the economy, something that maybe your portfolio managers are saying and identifying and comparisons in the economy.

You want to look at those three to five bullet points and say this, "This is important because..." Then you're going to get an answer.

**By simply asking yourself "This is important because..." you start opening up your mind to the reasons of why that's important.**

Then, if that's not a good reason why, you keep going until you feel like you get to the deeper level. You get under the surface level of what you're going to tell them. You say, "This is important because..." and start generating deeper reasons of why it's important, of what you want to say.

By simply asking yourself "This is important because..." you start opening up your mind to the reasons of why that's important.

That's really simply how to start with your why.

## Putting It All Together

The idea is when you put your reasons why in front of what you want to say in front of how you do it, ultimately what you're going to do is increase your persuasion.

You're going to get people to pay attention a lot more, and what I say is you're going to have a Scooby Doo affect. If you remember the Scooby Doo cartoon, whenever Scooby Doo is interested he would make that funny noise.

He'd go, "Aroo," and so what you want to do is have that Scooby Doo affect with your audience, and how you do that is by starting with why.

- What are the reasons why they should listen?
- What's the x-factor of your product?
- What's the yes set that you could utilize – basically three questions that they say yes to?
- A universal quantifier, that'd be three statements that they would say yes to
- Then building your why is simply look at the bullet points of what you want to say and ask yourself.

Go out there and start with why, utilize the reasons before what you want to say. It's a very simple technique.

It's a simple technique to use. It's a little bit harder to grasp, so what I really encourage you to do is how I learned soft skills, is I go out there and practice them for three, four, five days.

I'll practice them in my head when I'm driving around in the car.

**What I really encourage you to do to learn soft skills is to go out there and practice.**

I'll practice them with the Maître d' at a restaurant, the hostess at a restaurant, anybody I talk with.

I will start and practice putting the reasons why before what I ultimately want from them.

Go out there and practice starting with why.

Hit people's limbic brain and you'll be more successful and, like Martin Luther King got all those people to Washington and follow his "I have a dream" speech, you're going to be more impactful, more persuasive, and you're going to make more sales.

# Chapter 6

## Using 3-D Communication to Get the Message Across

3D COMMUNICATION ABOUT IS LISTENING CLOSELY TO THE OTHER PERSON.

It's then about delivering a message that is encoded in the types of words that make the most sense to him or her.

It's like jumping from an old school television set to a high-definition flat screen television; from a reel-to-reel movie to seeing Avatar in 3D.

Do you remember the first time that you saw a high-definition television? I bet you do.

- The picture appeared crisp and defined.

- The bright colors were magical.
- You felt like you could reach out and touch the characters on screen.
- The image almost seemed like another world.

How about those of you who saw Avatar for the first time in 3D? When I watched it, it looked so real that I had to periodically lift up my glasses and check in with reality. I bet you did too. (You can admit it. I won't tell anyone.)

**3D Communication is understanding communication styles and using that to communicate the most effective way possible.**

Whatever you felt, saw, or heard that first time is exactly what I am talking about when it comes to communication.

3D communication is similar to seeing a movie in HD or 3D. It brings clarity to the linguistic process.

It's the process of understanding communication styles and using that knowledge to communicate in the most advanced, effective way possible.

Using 3D linguistically is a win-win situation for all who are involved.

In Neuro-Linguistic Programming (NLP) this concept is defined using representational systems. Representational systems are our chosen methods of processing information through one of our five senses.

A simple example of this involves my wife and myself.

- She is adept at visual processing, and will often say, "I look at this..." or "I see that..."

- On the other hand, I am most comfortable as a kinesthetic processor, and I will say, "I feel this..." or "I feel that..."

The funny thing is, until we realized this concept, we used to drive each other absolutely crazy.

The point is, while all humans process information through their senses, we all process it differently.

Here's a breakdown of our sensory-based information styles (VAKOG):

- Visual – Sight
- Auditory – Hearing
- Kinesthetic – Touch
- Olfactory – Smell
- Gustatory – Taste

**The point is, while all humans process information through their senses, we all process it differently.**

In the field of NLP, we believe most people - and most circumstances - use three of the five sensory-based modes in mental processing. Most people use Visual, Auditory and Kinesthetic (VAK).

In the appendix at the back of this book, is a quick test to help discover what representational system you favor.

As you quickly learn your own, and start to master other people's representational systems, you will become a 3D communicator.

There's one method that can help you become well-versed in using other people's representational systems.

When possible, when you are communicating, write down everything you can as the other person talks.

Then, when you are delivering your message, implement their key words into your delivery.

Here is the process:

1. Listen for key words
2. Write down the key words
3. Utilize the key words when delivering your content

For example, one day I realized that my wife repeatedly used words and phrases such as "mind's eye" or "I see it this way."

So I started using those words back to her, and suddenly we were communicating on the same level.

Yes, you may feel funny or insecure about doing this. But trust me – the other person will not even notice.

Make sure to use all the modalities in your stories.

# Chapter 7

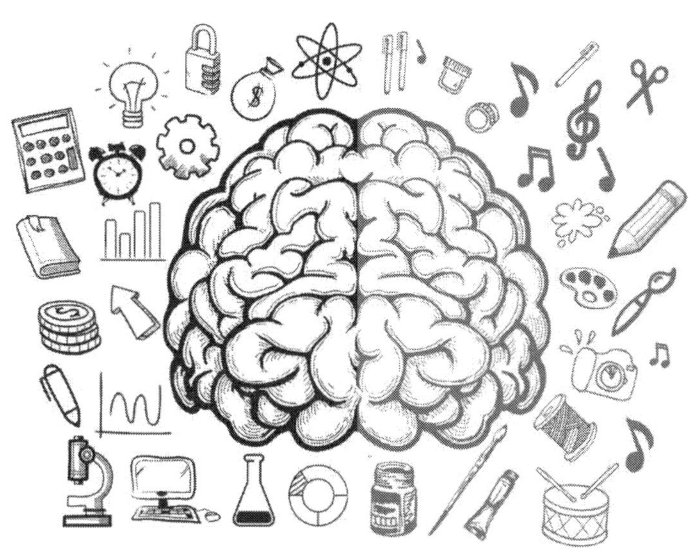

## How to Construct a Powerful Story or Metaphor

NOW THAT WE'VE COVERED A LOT OF THE BUILDING BLOCKS, WE'RE READY TO CREATE STORIES THAT WORK.

In this segment, I want to share with you how to construct a metaphor – a powerful story that helps you be more persuasive.

So what is a metaphor?

I am going to use a couple of different definitions to explain the full picture.

Webster says:

> ***met•a•phor (noun)***
>
> *A figure of speech in which a word for one idea or thing is used in place of another to suggest a likeness between them.*

But my own definition for professional use focuses more on getting what you want by skillfully bypassing the critical faculty:

> ***met•a•phor (noun)***
>
> *A story used for the purpose of creating change in someone, or allowing them to listen in hi-definition, thus allowing them to see something in a new light, feel something different or hear in a way they never have heard.*

So you can see that the most powerful stories are not just fun. They have the purpose of changing beliefs and behavior.

## Breaking the Barrier

For example, go back to the Jack Nicklaus story I shared on page 11. I've been using that story for about years.

I use it almost every time I speak, every time I do a training, every time I do a seminar, and here's why.

What I want to do is ultimately connect with the audience. It helps me connect. It helps me get them laughing. It opens up their mind and bypasses their critical faculty barrier.

The truth is you cannot disagree with a story or metaphor. It just is what it is. You're just listening to be entertained almost.

A metaphor allows us to break through the client's critical faculty barrier, or mental block.

As we discussed earlier, the critical faculty barrier is our resistance that makes us see circumstances simply as they appear versus what they could be.

Thus, our projection (or resultant behavior) is our perception of circumstances.

Metaphors can skillfully move past and sneak around the critical faculty barrier.

By utilizing the techniques that I have laid out for you in this book, the abstract can become specific and concrete.

**Metaphors can skillfully move past and sneak around the critical faculty barrier.**

Metaphors can make the complicated easy. Metaphors can provide the discomfort that influences the decision for change.

**The most powerful stories have the purpose of changing beliefs and behavior.**

Great orators of the past, present and future have all been great storytellers. Think of your favorite. Do they tell a great story? How do they communicate?

I have seen and given many presentations over many years, and what all great presenters have in common is the ability to tell a great story.

Keep in mind why we do this in a professional setting – we may think what we do or say is the most interesting thing ever, but I promise your material is not nearly as interesting as you are.

Wrapping a story around it makes it, at the very least, tolerable to the audience and may even influence, elicit or effect change.

Isn't this our goal in many business and interpersonal communications?

We want people to agree with our point of view. I know I do.

## Constructing the Metaphor

So let's talk about the actual process for constructing a metaphor.

Here are the key steps to effectively use a metaphor to break through the critical faculty barrier:

1. Change a client's personal reference to a character in the story.
2. Pace the client's situation by linking behaviors and events between the characters in the story and the client's situation.
3. Find resources for the client within the context of the story.
4. Make sure the story features events in which the characters re-solve the conflict and achieve the desired outcome.

Let me explain using the example of the Jack Nicklaus story I shared on page 11.

### #1. Change Personal Reference

The first step in the process is you want to change the client's personal reference to a character in the story.

So when I tell that story, I aim to change the personal reference of the audience to Jack Nicklaus.

When I change them over to Jack Nicklaus, they are thinking, "Jack's a successful guy. I'm a successful guy or lady."

Then I say, "The king wanted Jack to come and play golf."

This ties in with you coming to my seminar or you came to my training.

Now this is going to sound arrogant but this isn't egotistical... I try to set the reference that, "You're Jack, you're successful and I'm the king. I'm going to help you think bigger and help you push to new heights."

We start setting the chains to personal reference through a character in the story. That's my intention.

### 2. Pace the Client by Linking Behaviors

Next step is to pace the client by linking behaviors.

So maybe you didn't want to come to my training or my seminar. Maybe you were told to come or you were dragged along and you're like, "Ah, I don't know."

They said, "Hey, don't worry. The company's paying for it."

So I'm aiming to pace the client by linking behaviors.

**3. Find Resources**

Then I want to find resources for my audience within the story.

The resources are, "Jack's thinking a golf club, but the king is thinking a 500-acre golf club."

**4. Resolve Conflict**

The final step is that I want to resolve the conflict.

The conflict in that situation is people not wanting to be there.

So I want to start putting the audience at ease to make my job easier.

Ultimately, I just want them to open up their minds that they're here to be motivated, to think bigger, and have better results for their life.

That's the idea of that metaphor.

My brother came and spent some days with me recently. He said, "Wow, listening to your audios and your tapes, you tell a lot of stories. I just noticed all this."

I said, "Nothing is by accident. Everything is told for a specific reason."

## Pre-Steps

Here are some of the pre-steps to creating a metaphor.

1. Identify behavior and events
2. Determine the strategy that's in question that they're currently utilizing
3. Pinpoint the desired outcomes that you ultimately want them to have

You want to identify the behavior in the person or people you are trying to communicate with, whether one person or many.

What is the behavior or what is their current belief or what are they currently doing that you want to change?

Once you identify that behavior, then you want to determine which strategy they are utilizing that you want to put into question.

You identify their behavior, but then they're doing some kind of strategy or implementing some type of belief.

You want to determine that strategy that you think is in question for them and could cause problems to them and that's the solution you're going to provide.

Then you ultimately want to pinpoint the desired outcomes you want for them.

It's some kind of a belief. It's something that you want them to change the way they're doing something; the way they believe about something.

## Mapping Strategies

Next part of the process is simple mapping strategies.

1. Displace referential characters

   A. Establish Characters
   B. Preserve Relationship
2. Establish a connection between the client's current situation or behavior, and the characters' situation and behaviors
3. Establish resources of the characters and events
4. Resolution
   A. Ambiguous
   B. Direct Connect

### 1. Displacing Referential Characters

What you want to do is displace the referential characters.

You want to displace your audience with the characters in this story because if you come straight at them and say, "Hey, I had this similar problem. This is what I did. This is how it happened," then they know that you're trying to sell them, even if it's in your personal life with your husband or your wife or your kids.

They know because you are not displacing the character.

You're not just telling them a metaphor openly, like the Golden Bear story I told.

You want to make sure you're displacing the referential characters to maintain the relationship. Because if you say, "Here, this is how you're acting," well, then they're going to say, "I'm not acting that way."

### 2. Establishing Connection

Number two is you want to establish connection between the client and the character.

You want to establish connection between the client's behavior, the character's behavior, the client's strategy, the character's strategy, and ultimately you want to establish a connection to the outcome.

### 3. Establish Resources

You establish those resources as we talked about.

- What are some resources that the character used?
- What are some resources that the character established?
- What are some of the resources that the character left the story with?

Jack Nicklaus, he went to the king. Jack's a successful guy. The resources were that he went and played. He spent time with somebody.

Because of his spending time with somebody, he actually started thinking a little bit bigger at the end because he was thinking golf club and the king was thinking 500-acre golf club.

### 4. Resolution

Lastly, the resolution is when you're done telling the story.

Depending on the situation, you may want to connect the story directly to the client's situation, or leave the metaphor ambiguous for the client to make connections at an unconscious level.

You could leave the story to be ambiguous, meaning that at the end of the Jack Nicklaus story, I could say, "The king sent the letter and in the letter was a deed for a 500-acre golf club," and then I could have moved on right to the next point.

Or I could say, "You see the king thinks a lot bigger than Jack." You can leave it ambiguous or have a direct connection.

## Recipe

Lastly, here's your recipe. This is how you get it.

**Recipe for a Solid Metaphor**

1. Find a story, namely a piece from your past that had an impact on you.
2. Read it over or go over it once mentally.
3. Let it cook in your mind overnight.
4. Read it or go over it mentally again.
5. Let it cook overnight again in your mind.
6. Deliver the story.

You want to find a story, a slice of life. Something that may have happened to you in the past or something that you felt a connection to.

Either you enjoyed the story, you thought it was funny, or you had an emotional connection to it.

Next, you want to read it over. You either want to write it out or you want to have the story that maybe you got out of a book, but you want to be able to read it over.

What I say is you want to let it cook for one day and at least overnight.

You let it cook in your mind so you can really rehearse it and make sure that you are pacing and leading the client with the characters, with the current problems the character has, and you're pacing and leading them through the success.

When you let something cook overnight, your unconscious mind goes to work and helps you formulate the plan.

Again, the next day you want to read it over again.

Let it cook overnight one more time, so you're letting it cook for two nights.

Then you deliver it.

Obviously, in business, before you use a metaphor, you want to let it cook those two days, but then when you deliver it, you're going to continuously deliver that story and that metaphor and utilize it for your business.

**When you let something cook overnight, your unconscious mind goes to work and helps you formulate the plan.**

## Telling Stories

I'll tell you what. Just because you're in front of the same audience, say one time, two times, three times, five times, it's okay to use the same story and here's why.

Because every time you use that story, it takes on a different meaning.

Have you ever watched a movie, say, five years ago, you watch it again and you're like, "Wow, that's a lot better movie"? Or you had a different thought about that movie? Or you didn't realize that that movie had that type of outcome?

Ultimately it's because your perception is your projection. You might have heard of that before. Your audience's perception is their projection.

They're grabbing onto different parts of that story and pieces of that story at all times.

Whether you're using that in a one-on-one situation or you're utilizing it with an audience, don't be afraid to use the story more than once with the same audience.

That's how you deliver a metaphor in a story. I encourage you to start implementing this into your communication and you'll have more success and be more persuasive.

Now we have the formula of how to build a metaphor.

> **You may want to have pre-constructed metaphors for situations that keep repeating themselves.**

In business, I often see two varying situations where developing a metaphor is useful.

In addition, you may want to have pre-constructed metaphors for situations that keep repeating themselves, as we often stumble upon the same sets of circumstances.

Keep in mind that once you tell the story it will be different the next time and every time after that.

## Metaphor Examples

Here are a few examples of how metaphors work:

<u>Situation A</u>

This situation happens when you are presented with an outright problem for which you need to find a resolution.

Figure 1 puts together everything we have mentioned so far.

We are presented with a problem and we need to move over to a solution.

The gap is the trip from the problem to the solution.

The bridge from the problem to the solution is the metaphor.

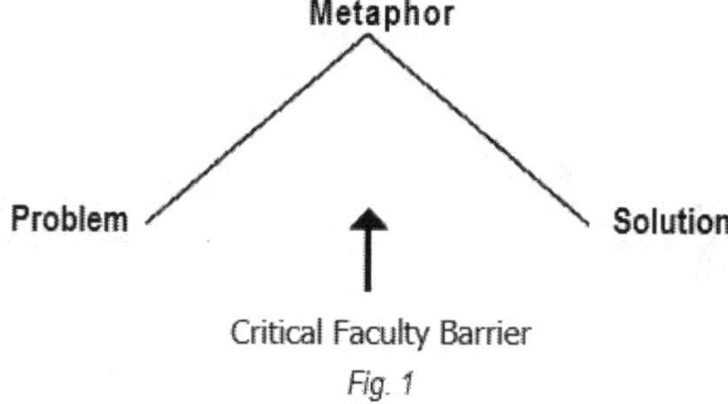


*Fig. 1*

The metaphor massages the tight hold the client has on their model of the world, which makes their actions more difficult than they should be.

This massage will allow you to morph the problem from their current behavior into the solution or product set that you provide.

Figure 2 leads us down the path to find the metaphor. You will see now how to implement the chunking exercise.

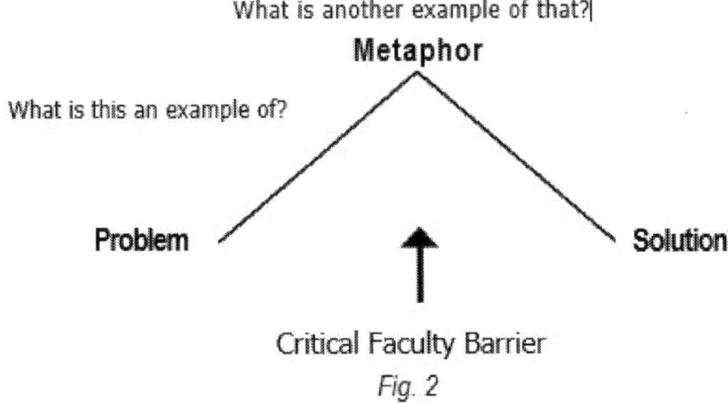

*Fig. 2*

When you become adept at building pre-planned metaphors as instructed by the process above, you will become unconsciously competent with your ability.

You will not have to think so critically hard. You've learned something like this before, haven't you?

Unconscious competence is the last step in the four-step learning process.

When we learn, we move from present state, or unconscious incompetence, to unconscious competence, demonstrated by the diagram here.

**Present State**

1st step is **unconscious incompetence**
*We don't know what we don't know.*

2nd step is **conscious incompetence**
*We know we don't know.*

3rd step is **conscious competence**
*We know that we know.*

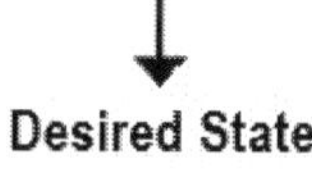

4th step is **unconscious competence**
*We forget what we know, but we still know.*

Learning at first can seem painfully frustrating, but in the end it is very rewarding.

Situation B

This is mostly done in sales or to open up presentations, as we are rarely presented with an outright problem from the client or prospect.

But we know that our product or service solves a particular problem. (At least, I hope you know what needs your product or service satisfies.)

So we need to develop a metaphor to illustrate a problem that our client does not even notice they have until our product or service is a recommended solution.

Figure 3 illustrates how this works.

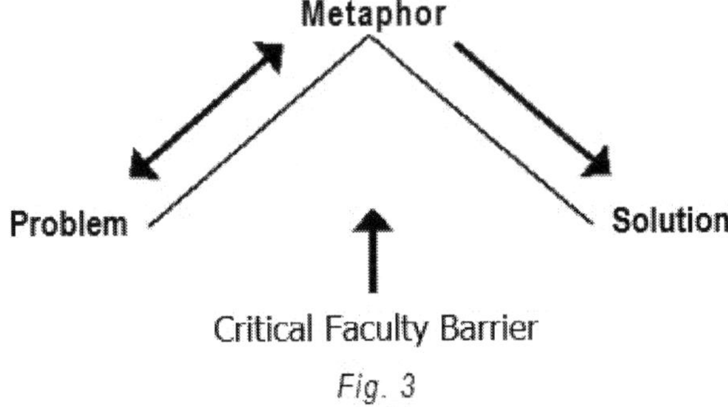


*Fig. 3*

When we are communicating with somebody, they may not even realize they have a problem.

They may not realize they could be doing their work more efficiently or more cost-effectively.

During a presentation, I find it best to begin with a metaphor that opens up a problem.

I hone the audience's mind to an idea or a problem that will resonate with them.

Next, I describe how my product can be an efficient way to solve the problem that's now at the forefront of their mind, since I put it there. Figure 4 illustrates how to do this.

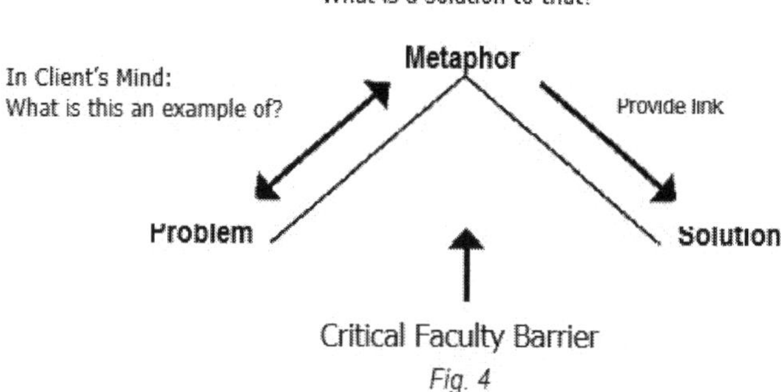


*Fig. 4*

# Chapter 8

## Using Reframing to Change Minds

IN EFFECTIVE COMMUNICATION, KNOWING HOW TO REFRAME IS EXTREMELY IMPORTANT.

> **By changing the context one can change the meaning of almost any method of communication.**

Reframing allows you to change the context or meaning of a word or sentence.

Since all interpretation is context dependent, by

changing the context, one can change the meaning of almost any method of communication.

When you reframe, you alter the meaning or value of something by changing the context or description.

Here's an easy example:

A 60-degree day can have two totally different meanings given the context:

- In my hometown of Chicago, after a long winter it is not unusual to see people wearing shorts the first time the temperature hits 60.
- But when we reframe that, we see that in Hawaii, people are wearing parkas when it's 60 degrees.

The great motivational speaker Anthony Robbins wrote, "A signal has meaning only in the frame or context in which we perceive it."

For example, if a person is resting in bed and hears his bedroom door open, that exact same noise will have two totally different meanings and evoke drastically different reactions depending on whether he is alone in a locked house, or if he had previously invited his friend over and left the back door to his house unlocked.

If we perceive something as a liability, that's the message we deliver to our brain, and then the brain produces states that make it a reality.

If we change our frame of reference by looking at the same situation from a different point of view, we can change the way we respond.

We can change our representation or perception about anything, and in a moment change our states and behaviors. This is what reframing is all about.

If you change the context, meaning or content, you can change the meaning of the situation, the idea being to separate intention from behavior.

I believe reframing is great to use when handling objections or negative behavior regarding a situation or circumstance.

There are two types of reframes:

- Context Reframe
- Meaning Reframe

**Context Reframe**

In a context reframe, you establish a different context in which the person will respond differently to the same behavior. The meaning of any behavior or event exists only in relationship to the context in which it occurs.

**If we change our frame of reference by looking at the same situation from a different point of view, we can change the way we respond.**

**Ask yourself, what is another context for this behavior where the meaning will be different?**

An example of this is one that I used in a training with an airline representative.

She said that she would love to have a reframe for unruly passengers, specifically when flights are delayed.

I asked her, "Are flights typically delayed because of weather?"

"Yes!" She responded emphatically.

So here's a possible reframe:

> *"Mr. or Mrs. Client, I completely understand your attitude. Last week I was traveling with my fiancé.*
>
> *The weather was horrible. He kept bugging me that we were going to be late because I was driving too slowly.*
>
> *I looked at him and said, 'I understand your frustration, but do you want to get there on time or do you want to get there safely?'"*

**Meaning Reframe**

In a meaning reframe, you take an undesired attribute and find a description where the attribute takes on a positive value.

In other words, "whenever x happens, I respond with y."

**Ask yourself what it is that this person hasn't noticed in this context that will bring about a different meaning and change his response?**

Meaning reframe is best illustrated by former President Bill Clinton, at his notorious impeachment proceedings.

In every question the prosecutor asked him, Clinton kept asking the prosecutor to define the word "is."

Was it a current relationship or a past relationship? What was the tense of the question? Each time, Clinton wanted to change the meaning of "is" to his benefit.

Another meaning reframe example comes from my childhood.

One of my brothers thought that because my mom really bugged him to get his chores and homework done, she therefore did not love him.

But I thought that, because mom made sure our chores and homework were done, she cared for us and wanted us to succeed in life – and have time to play.

In a more recent example, I was discussing sending Save the Date mailers with a couple who is getting married in the near future, and they were on complete opposite ends of the spectrum.

**In a meaning reframe, you take an undesired attribute and find a description where the attribute takes on a positive value.**

She wanted to spend the money on the mailers and he was absolutely opposed to the cost.

Within this conversation, I relayed the story of how recently I was sent a mailer by the United States Government, informing me that in a week I was going to receive a census request.

But with all the budget deficits, I thought that maybe the United States Government could have just sent the census to save money.

When focused on her Save the Dates, the bride couldn't see her fiancé's point of view, but when I reframed it to reference an entirely different situation (one that she was likely familiar with), she was able to see how he would think it was a waste of money.

Reframing is a powerful strategy you can use to make your communication more effective.

# Chapter 9

## Six Secrets of Influence That Will Transform Your Messages

NOW, I WANT TO SHARE WITH YOU THE SIX PRINCIPLES OF INFLUENCE TO MAKE YOUR MESSAGES MORE PERSUASIVE.

Whether you're trying to sell somebody on a product or sell somebody on an idea, we all know that we could use more persuasiveness in our messages.

Here are the six principles that are based on Robert Cialdini's book, "Influence." I recommend it. It's a great read. Go ahead and get it and go a little bit deeper.

In this chapter, let's get you well on your way to understanding the six principles of influence.

**What third party authorities can you bring in to build your credibility. Use authority in your messaging.**

## 1. Authority

The first one is "Authority." I worked for a few insurance companies over the years and they were always wanting us to put forth their awards and their rankings.

For instance, at one of the insurance companies they said, "We have great customer service. We won the DALBAR Award. You need to tell everybody."

Another company, we were the number one seller of annuities and they wanted us to tell everybody that we were the best.

Even now when I get introduced or I introduce myself, I love to tell the awards that I had won, because I love to tell people that I'm a bestselling author. I love this and then I'm a master and trainer and certified personal coach in neuro-linguistic programming.

All of this is really done just to build my authority. What can you do to build your authority or when you're presenting an idea, what third parties can you bring in to kind of build your credibility?

## 2. Consistency and Commitment

Number two is "Consistency and commitment." Now, I am not a gambler, but a couple of years ago, I did go to the Kentucky Derby. I was there with a Mastermind group and I did bet on some horses.

They were small bets, but after I made the bet, I was more certain that my horse was going to win. The consistency of my commitment drove up my belief.

In the South Korea War, they asked some POWs some questions about communism.

Then what they were able to do was get them in some sort of light to agree that communism isn't all that bad.

Maybe it's okay because essentially, they're supposed to have full employment. Everybody gets to eat, whatever it was.

But what they did is they took their messages and quoted the prisoners of war in the newspaper.

What happened is the other prisoners of war, their other counterparts couldn't believe that they said these things and the people that were quoted had to back it up and had to persuade them of what they said.

They had to stand by their commitment. They had to be consistent with what they said.

So how can you use consistency and commitment in your communication?

Another one is, what's the biggest commitment that you've ever made and what was your consistency of belief that followed it?

For example, just think about the most expensive thing you ever bought, whatever that might be, a car or a house. Think about how consistent you were with the belief after that.

If somebody ever told you anything that was contrary to what you just bought or the biggest action you just took, the biggest commitment you just made, you were probably more certain about your belief and stood by your belief even more.

**Social proof makes you feel more comfortable about what you are going to do.**

### 3. Social Proof

The third one is "Social proof." This adds a benefit for people who are uncertain how to act.

Have you ever been at maybe a wedding or somewhere where there was a buffet and you looked at the buffet and you said, "Hey, can we go eat now? Should we go eat now?"

You look at everybody else, "Well, is anyone else going to eat now?"

Then as soon as somebody went over there and ate, you got up and went to the buffet. "Well, they're going, I can go."

The social proof made you better able to act, made you feel more comfortable about what you were going to do.

How about infomercials online? They show these all the time. They show the social proof of how the product is going to work and then they'd get you to buy.

Maybe you haven't bought on infomercials, but the reality is, they work.

How do I know they work? It's because people keep doing them and they spend tens of thousands of dollars just to produce infomercials and sell hundreds and millions of dollars of product and it's all based on the social proof of the product.

### 4. Reciprocity

Number four is "Reciprocity." Now, we know that reciprocity is, "I do this for you, you're going to feel compelled to do it for me."

Here is a story. A boy scout was selling circus tickets, went up to a guy and said, "Hey, would like to buy some circus tickets?"

That's a big commitment. Let's say they're $100 circus tickets and the said, "Well one, that's $100. Two, that's a time commitment. I'm sorry little guy. I don't want to buy the circus tickets."

The boy scout comes back and says, "Okay. Well, there's no problem. How about buying some candy bars?"

The gentleman tells the story as he walked away with these chocolate candy bars and he didn't even like chocolate. It was all about the reciprocity and we call this the rejection and retreat.

If somebody rejects a bigger offer, you retreat to a lower offer and your compliance goes up. This is called the down-sell in sales.

I'm trying to go beyond what we typically think of as reciprocity... "I do this for you, you should feel compelled to do this for me."

You can also use this in the rejection, retreat and down-sell model.

## 5. Liking

The fifth principle is "Liking." We all think of liking as a common interest. You like Michigan State, I like Michigan State.

But the reality is, we make a decision in a split second of whether we like somebody or not and rapport is one of the keys to this.

How about good cop, bad cop? The guy comes in as being the bad, so it makes the other cop that much more likable.

Joe Girard is the number one sales person in the world by Guinness Book of World Records.

What he did to increase his liking is every month, he sent out a card to thirteen thousand people and all the card said on it was, "I like you."

This made Joe more likable and he had sold more cars than anybody in the history of selling cars.

## 6. Scarcity

The sixth one is "Scarcity." How do you use scarcity? Now, scarcity is simple as, "We only have ten of these left, or five of these left."

If you're selling a book, "We only printed fifty of these books. Go ahead and get this book now before they're all gone."

How about when you just think about scarce now versus always scarce? If something is always scarce, you don't really care... It doesn't really pique your interest as much as versus something that is scarce now.

Let's say your office never had chocolate chip cookies in it. You wouldn't think of chocolate chip cookies too often.

But let's say you had a jar of chocolate chip cookies and you knew they had thirteen cookies in there and there's thirteen people in your office. You know that you didn't have one of those cookies and a couple of hours later, there's one left.

How certain are you that you're going to go grab that last cookie before somebody else in your office takes two?

**It's all about creating that scarcity to make people take more action right now or action faster.**

The idea there is that always scarce versus scarce now is different.

If something was in abundance and now it's scarce, people have a higher compliance to want to take action.

Let's look at this. Do you have any kids, or when you were a kid, did your parents tell you that you couldn't date somebody?

You might not even have liked the person but, as soon as they told you you couldn't date them, you certainly went on more dates with that person.

It's all about creating that scarcity around yourself or around your product or whatever it is, to make people take more action right now or action faster.

Those are the six principles of influence that will help make your messages more persuasive.

Make sure you use all these principles in your stories.

# Chapter 10

## Creating Your Own Dream Story

FINALLY LET'S DISCUSS YOUR STORY AND HOW YOU CAN USE IT TO CHANGE YOUR LIFE.

It's important to know what story you are telling yourself.

- What's your story?
- What's your why?
- What drives you every day?

When you understand what's driving you, you can change the stories you tell yourself and use them to get better results in everything you do.

What happens in your life is ultimately about your story and your why that's going to drive you.

If you have a business or work in a business, it's the story of the business and the why that's going to drive your organization.

It's the story and your why that's going to drive your team.

So what is your why? What is your story that you're telling every day?

You see companies out there whose culture is like a cult, where people – employees and customers – have bought into the story.

Apple is one of the best known examples. Just talk to someone who works there or someone who buys their products.

It looks bizarre from the outside, doesn't it?

It's just because their why is so strong, their story is so strong. That's what driving them, that's what's driving their organization.

**When you understand what's driving you, you can change the stories you tell yourself.**

So what's driving you?

Let's identify what's your story right now.

## Decide Your Story

As you sit there reading this, I want you to close your eyes. I want you to think about what's your biggest dream.

- What's the biggest dream that you have for your career?
- What's the biggest dream that you have for your life?
- What's the biggest dream that you have for your business?

There is one caveat, it has to be a dream that you've not yet accomplished. It has to be a dream that maybe you've given up.

You remember that dream when you first started working or maybe you were a kid and you had this big, grandiose dream.

When you were a kid people smiled at you and said, "That's so cute, you could do anything."

As you grow older, they start looking at you and saying, "Oh honey, that's not how the world works."

Remember, it has to be a dream that you've not yet accomplished, a dream that you've given up on, or one of those dreams that every time you seem to get closer it seems that much further in future.

You know what I'm talking about. We all have those dreams.

- What's your biggest dream?
- What's your biggest dream that you've had for your life?
- What's the biggest dream that you've had for your career?
- What's the biggest dream you have for your business or organization and it just doesn't seem to be getting there?

I want you to close your eyes for a few moments, remember that dream and then come back and write it down here....

________________________________________

________________________________________

________________________________________

________________________________________

________________________________________

## What's Holding You Back

When you have that dream, what I want you write down is all the reasons that you've not yet accomplished it.

What are all the reasons that you've given up on that dream.

- "I procrastinate"
- "I'm too lazy"
- "I'm too tall"
- "I'm too short, too skinny, too fat..."

Write down all the reasons why you don't have that dream or that you've given up on it.

________________________________________

________________________________________

________________________________________

________________________________________

________________________________________

As you have a few things down there what I want you to do is circle them, put a line through them and write "BS" over the top. This is your BS.

You're like a boat which can go anywhere in the world. This ship can go anywhere but what steers it is the rudder.

What steers you is your BS, your belief system. Your belief system acts like the rudder for your life. Your belief system is the story you're telling yourself.

The belief system for your organization is the story you're telling your organization.

The belief system for the people that you're leading is the story that you're telling them.

## Changing Direction

> **If you change the direction of a boat by just one degree, soon it's going 180 degrees in the opposite direction.**

So how do you keep pushing your story, how do you keep pushing so you can change the direction of your life, the direction of your organization, the direction of your team?

It's just changing your 'why' a little bit.

If you change the direction of a boat by just one degree, soon it's going 180 degrees in the opposite direction.

It's just about how do you change that belief system.

How do we change beliefs?

We change belief through stories.

You have to change your story.

You have to change your why.

If you've ever heard of a plane's envelope before, a plane's envelope is the limitations put on a plane by science and math.

Great aeronautical engineers of all time, great pilots of all time, try to push a plane's envelope.

See we all live in our own self-deductive envelope. It's driven by our belief system.

It's driven by our story.

It's driven by our why.

## 50/50 Beliefs

If your belief system is 50/50, "I think we can but we need a plan B." Plan A sounds good but what's plan B? Some people even have plan C, D and E.

A 50/50 belief system is, "Let's give it a try. If it doesn't work, we'll try something else."

**If you start taking 50/50 actions your results are going to be 50/50.**

If you have a 50/50 belief system, what kind of potential do you have?

50/50.

What kind of actions are you going to take if you have a 50/50 potential?

50/50.

You're going to go in and say, "Hey, I'm going to persuade these guys. I'm going to tell them."

You go in to the board of directors and they say, "Hey you know, we gave you twenty minutes but we only have five minutes." Then you say, "Why did I even try?"

Then that's the results you have.

So if you start taking 50/50 actions your results are going to be 50/50 and you're going to say, "Why did we try?"

We all spin this same cycle.

As individuals, as teams, as organizations, information comes in from the outside and we spin the same cycle.

## Expanding Your Why

How do we keep expanding our envelope and keep building our story, building our personal why and building our team's why to push the envelope each and every day?

How do you keep expanding your why, developing your why, developing your story, crafting your story, changing it by one degree so you... your life, your team, your organization... are going 180 degrees in the opposite direction – the direction that you wrote down above.

What happens is this, we all live in a gray zone.

What's going to happen is you're going to say, "Oh man, that was really fun, this was a great book. That Matt guy is awesome."

Then you're going to say I'm going to use stories.

Then you go back to your computer and you've got 100 emails. "I'm going to do it this weekend, I'm going to spend an hour, oh I'm going to have a beer."

We live in this gray zone and we never change, we never push, we never develop our why, we never develop our story.

Bad habits are hard to stop.

Great habits are hard to start.

How do we push our gray zones?

We don't change until we meet a vitrification point where things get so bad we're propelled to a new order.

My dad is 6'2" and he weighed 350 pounds. He did not lose weight until he moved down to Florida and blew up with water and his medicine stopped working.

He was propelled to a new order. He didn't change his why, he didn't change his story, he didn't change until things got so bad that he had to.

**If you could just start with your why, you soon will push your envelope and be on to new levels of success.**

That's what teams do, don't they?

We get comfortable, we get comfortable as leaders, we get comfortable in our household, our family's okay.

It's hard to set a new standard, it's hard to change our leadership style but if you could just start with your why, you soon will push your envelope and be on to new levels of success.

Elevate your standard each and every day and elevate your team standard each and every day.

If you live at a high standard your team is going to live at a high standard.

If you live at a high standard your origination's going to be at a high standard.

Remember people don't play to their potential. They play to the standard that you set for them.

## Four Things That Get In Your Way

There are four things that get in your way and that get in your team's way.

**Your Mind**

Number one is your mind. We always think we need more – we need more money, we need more head count, we can't do this, we need more.

You have to get started at some point, it's not about having more. It's not about knowing everything, it's about creating a story that helps you get over that and get started.

**Your Body**

Number two is your body. Your body gets in the way and this also applies to the organization.

In my offices you can't bring in fast food, you've got to eat healthy.

The reason is your body's going to get in the way. We're crafting a story to have a ton of energy.

We're crafting our why to be able to push a little bit further than the day before.

We just want to push a little bit further every day.

So one thing that gets in your way is your body.

That's usually you're not eating right, you're not exercising, you're not creating tons of energy.

So how do you create tons of energy within your team, how do you create tons of energy within your life and how do you create tons of energy within in your family?

**Your Emotions**

Next is your emotions. Do you ever say to yourself, "Why do I always do this? Why does this always happen this way? Why do I always say that?"

Our emotions get in the way. Not to be ethereal here but a lot of people meditate now.

Schultz at Starbucks talks about meditating; Bezos at Amazon talks about meditating, Ariana Huffington talks about meditating.

If you just sit in silence for five to twenty minutes a day, you'll start developing your new why. New ideas will come to you.

> **If you can meditate on what you ultimately want, you can craft a better story.**

If you can meditate on what you ultimately want, you can craft a better story, you're going to craft a better why.

So take time and stillness and new ideas will come to you.

**Your Environment**

Another thing is environment gets in your way, "Oh, it would be better if we had more this or the company would be better if they just let us do this."

Here's the problem with the environment.

Let's just say you're overweight and you want to lose some weight.

You say, "I'm overweight because McDonald's in on the corner. I'm going to move."

Guess who's still there when you move.

You.

If your team's not where it wants to be, it's not the environment. It's you.

It's not that it can't be a toxic environment but you have to think about:

- How does my story become better than my environment?
- How does my why push beyond my environment?
- How does my why lead this environment to a new level of success?

What's your story, what's your why, what's driving you every day.

What's driving your organization, what's driving your team?

It's all the story, it's all what your beliefs are and it's all the why behind it.

If you can just push your envelope, change the direction of your belief system by just one degree for you, your life, your organization, your team and your family, you soon will be going 180 degrees in the opposite direction and on your way to accomplishing whatever those things are that you wrote down above.

I encourage you to start now.

## Summary of Metaphor Creation

### Constructing the Metaphor

1. Change a client's personal reference to a character in the story.
2. Pace the client's situation by linking behaviors and events between the characters in the story and the client's situation.
3. Find resources for the client within the context of the story.
4. Make sure the story features events in which the characters re-solve the conflict and achieve the desired outcome.

### Pre-steps

1. Identify behavior and events
2. Determine the strategy that's in question that they're currently utilizing
3. Pinpoint the desired outcomes that you ultimately want them to have

## Mapping strategies

1. Displace referential characters
   A. Establish Characters
   B. Preserve Relationship
2. Establish a connection between the client's current situation or behavior, and the characters' situation and behaviors
3. Establish resources of the characters and events
4. Resolution
   A. Ambiguous
   B. Direct Connect

## Recipe for a Solid Metaphor

1. Find a story, namely a piece from your past that had an impact on you.
2. Read it over or go over it once mentally.
3. Let it cook in your mind overnight.
4. Read it or go over it mentally again.
5. Let it cook overnight again in your mind.
6. Deliver the story.

# Million Dollar Metaphor Library

IN THIS SEGMENT, YOU'LL FIND A FEW EXAMPLES OF MY PERSONAL FAVORITE METAPHORS.

They've proven successful in a variety of workplace situations.

It is a great thing to be able to deliver metaphors and reframes on the spot. This knowledge will help you to become a more persuasive communicator.

My hope is that everyone who will ever come across the knowledge in this book will realize the power contained within, and that we will be that much more effective in delivering our message because we now have new insights and understandings of communication.

You will enjoy your daily communications that much more because of your newly discovered knowledge.

People will remark upon how well you deliver your messages each and every day.

As you sit here reading, you don't realize that you know more than you think you know.

You will soon surprise yourself by using this knowledge with an unconscious competence.

Now go out with confidence, use your new skills and be a more effective communicator, wherever and whenever you wish.

# The Benefits of a Strong Running Game

Football is a game of great strategy. It is often said that offense draws crowds and defense wins championships, but that said, there are many different offensive philosophies when it comes to football.

While different schools of thought place importance in different areas, it is clear that everyone sees the value in a strong running game.

Every football team in America wants a reliable running back to control the ball and control the game.

A key component to winning is being the team who controls the clock by keeping their offense on the field and the opposing team's offense off the field.

A coach's dream is to have a running back who can consistently get over 3.3 yards per carry.

If the running back can accomplish this every three downs, the offense will have a fresh set of downs and continue their march down the field to the end zone.

Now, let's break down this anecdote with what we know so far.

**Metaphor Points of Construction**

1. Change a client's personal reference to a character in the story.
    A. Client's reference to offense in football
2. Pace the client's situation by linking behaviors and events between the characters in the story and the client's situation.
    A. Being consistent like a running back

3. Find resources for the client within the context of the story.
    A. Having a strategy
4. Make sure the story features events in which the characters in the story resolve the conflict and achieve the desired outcome.
    A. Strong offensive strategy wins the game

**Pre-Steps**

1. Identify behavior and events
    A. No strategy
2. Determine the strategy in question
    A. Game plan
3. Pinpoint desired outcomes
    A. Implement a game plan

**Mapping Strategies**

1. Displace referential characters
    A. Establish characters (e.g. the running back, etc.)
    B. Preserve relationship
2. Establish a connection between the client's current situation or behavior and the characters' situation or behaviors.
3. Establish resources of the characters and events.
    A. Consistency
4. Resolution
    A. Ambiguous
        i. Leave it the way the story reads now.
    B. Direct Connect
        i.

ring the story full circle, explaining how the current strategy is not successful like the consistent running back.

(Depending on the situation, you may want to either directly connect the story to the client's story, or leave the metaphor ambiguous for the client to make connections at an unconscious level.)

## Hitting for the Cycle Sales Idea

Who is your favorite baseball team?

Who was the last person to hit for the cycle on that team?

Hitting for the cycle is an extremely hard thing to do. In baseball, hitting for the cycle is when one player hits a single, double, triple and home run in a single game.

Why is this so hard? An average player gets about four to five at bats a game, and the best players only get one hit per every three at bats.

So to hit for the cycle, a player needs to get four hits in a single game.

In addition, the player has to get one of four possible hits in a single game. This requires the player to have a perfect combination of speed, power and luck to accomplish this momentous task.

In fact, since 1882, only 276 players have accomplished this feat in the major leagues.

Benefit 1: SINGLE

Benefit 2: DOUBLE

Benefit 3: TRIPLE

Benefit 4: HOME RUN

I use this metaphor in a couple different settings. In the first one, I explain that the company I work for hit for the cycle in producing the product I'm selling.

I do this by explaining four key benefits.

In the second setting, I use this to explain four key attributes someone needs to be as successful as a player who hits for the cycle.

Below is a breakdown of the latter example:

**Metaphor Points of Construction**

1. Change a client's personal reference to a character in the story.
    A. Target reference to baseball player
2. Pace the client's situation by linking behaviors and events be-tween the characters in the story and the client's situation.
    A. Having four attributes for success
3. Find resources for the client within the context of the story. A. Hitting for the cycle: a single, double, triple, home run
4. Make sure the story features events in which the characters in the story resolve the conflict and achieve the desired outcome.
    A. Make the impossible possible.

**Pre-Steps**

1. Identify behavior and events
    A. Four key attributes
2. Strategy in question
    A. Four key attributes
3. Desired outcomes
    A. Four key attributes

**Mapping Strategies**

1. Displace referential characters.
    A. Establish characters (e.g., baseball player, etc.)
    B. Preserve relationship

2. Establish a connection between the client's current situation or behavior, and the characters' situations or behaviors.
3. Establish resources of the characters and events.
    A. Player, four key attributes
4. Resolution
    A. Ambiguous
        i. Leave it the way the story reads now.
    B. Direct Connect
        i. Bring the story full circle to explain how the current strategy is not successful, like a baseball player hitting for the cycle.

# Wearing your Helmet

Who is your favorite professional baseball player?

Have you ever seen him go up to bat without a helmet on?

Of course you haven't. That would be crazy.

Have you ever seen him get hit in the head?

Well, let me review some statistics.

The average starting major league baseball player will have 400 at bats over the course of a full season.

On average, he will be hit by a pitch about eight times, or roughly 2 percent of his at bats in any given season. The chances that a player will be hit in the head by a pitch are less than 0.5 percent.

Getting hit in the head by a pitch is a nearly a statistical impossibility. But at the same time, you never see anyone step up to the plate without wearing a helmet.

**Metaphor Points of Construction**

1. Change a client's personal reference to a character in the story.
    A. Target reference to baseball player
2. Pace the client's situation by linking behaviors and events between the characters in the story and the client's situation.
    A. Being cautious
3. Find resources for the client within the context of the story.
    A. A baseball player

# Starbucks

Around 1972, a small coffee maker in Seattle, Washington named Starbucks was trying to increase the company's sales with an extremely limited marketing budget.

At the time they offered just a limited menu of drinks, all served in either a tall or venti size cup. The tall was their number one seller.

Most customers just couldn't fathom drinking an entire venti.

The venti appeared to be way too much coffee when positioned next to the tall.

With a limited marketing budget, Starbucks had the idea to implement the grande size drink in an attempt to increase coffee sales and consumption.

Quickly thereafter, the grande became the number one seller, taking over the tall size's popularity. The venti stepped in and took the number two spot.

The reality is that when an individual is confronted with three choices, they will almost always pick the middle option, or the perceived middle option, which in this case is the grande.

In conjunction, suddenly the venti did not seem so large when positioned next to the grande. Thus the grande became the best-seller and the venti became the number two best seller.

With that result Starbucks was able to increase their sales. It was a small change that yielded big results.

This story can be used in many facets in business.

## Metaphor Points of Construction

1. Change a client's personal reference to a character in the story.
    A. Client's reference is changed to Starbucks.
2. Pace the client's situation by linking behaviors and events be-tween the characters in the story and the client's situation.
    A. Having limited money but thinking resourcefully
3. Find resources for the client within the context of the story.
    A. Starbucks, budget, marketing intellect
4. Make sure the story features events in which the characters in the story resolve the conflict and achieve the desired outcome.
    A. Creative thinking

## Pre-Steps

1. Identify behavior and events
    A. Creativity, small change = big results
2. Strategy in question
    A. Limited budget
3. Desired outcomes
    A. New strategies

## Mapping Strategies

1. Displace referential characters.
    A. Establish characters (e.g., Starbucks, etc.)
    B. Preserve relationship
2. Establish a connection between the client's current situation or behavior and the characters' situations or behaviors.
3. Establish resources of the characters and events.

   A. Starbucks, strategy, small change = big results

4. Resolution
   A. Ambiguous
      i. Leave it the way the story reads now.
   B. Direct Connect
      i. Bring the story full circle, explaining how the current strategy needs to be revamped to brainstorm for ideas.

# The Triple Cheese

Nine years ago I started my illustrious career in the financial services industry as a stockbroker at Olde Discount.

It was an aggressive experience. There were twenty young guys packed into close quarters working a stressful job. Needless to say, a lot of fights and challenges started up on a daily basis in this testosterone-filled environment.

I witnessed sprinting contests, push-up duels and water cooler drinking competitions. But by far my favorite was the triple cheeseburger challenge. Here's what happened:

An office advisor was challenged to eat as many McDonald's triple cheeseburgers as he could. Clocking in at 5' 10", 260 pounds, the gentleman was a formidable foe for those burgers.

There was money on both sides, but he demolished five of those burgers in just minutes. (Full disclosure: He was laid up for the rest of the afternoon on a couch in the back room.)

I don't recommend anyone eating even one of these triple cheeseburgers, let alone five. But why would McDonald's even have them on the menu? They had a goal to sell more double cheeseburgers!

The problem started when they added the double cheeseburger to the menu. The double just seemed too large in comparison to the single cheeseburger.

By adding the triple next to the double on the menu, suddenly the double cheeseburger did not seem so large.

The result? The double cheeseburger is now the number one seller – and they still sold some triple cheeseburgers to guys like my colleague.

## Metaphor Points of Construction

1. Change a client's personal reference to a character in the story.
   A. Client's reference to McDonald's
2. Pace the client's situation by linking behaviors and events between the characters in the story and the client's situation.
   A. McDonald's trying to sell more double cheeseburgers
3. Find resources for the client within the context of the story.
   A. McDonald's and selling strategy
4. Make sure the story features events in which the characters in the story resolve the conflict and achieve the desired outcome.
   A. Sales increase

## Pre-Steps

1. Identify behavior and events
   A. Creativity, small change = big results
2. Strategy in question
   A. Creativity
3. Desired outcomes
   A. New strategies, increased sales

## Mapping Strategies

1. Displace referential characters.
   A. Establish characters (e.g., McDonald's, etc.)
   B. Preserve relationship

2. Establish a connection between the client's current situation or behavior and the characters' situations or behaviors.
3. Establish resources of the characters and events.
    A. Strategy, small change = big results
4. Resolution
    A. Ambiguous
        i. Leave it the way the story reads now.
    B. Direct Connect
        i. Bring the story full circle and explain how the current strategy needs to increase brainstorming for ideas.

# Coca-Cola

Around 1950, Coca-Cola was trying to figure out how to sell more soda (or "pop" if you're a Midwesterner).

They wanted people to either drink more Coca-Cola, or figure out how to lure away the consumers of other soda companies.

To learn more about their clients, they brought in a room full of people and divided them into soda drinkers and non-soda drinkers.

Right away they found they could not convert the non-soda drinkers into soda drinkers.

They just didn't like the taste, or they avoided soda for health reasons. So they kicked the non-soda drinkers out of the room.

Now, they were left with a room full of soda drinkers. So they divided them into Pepsi and Coca-Cola drinkers. They found they could not convert Pepsi drinkers into Coca-Cola drinkers.

The Pepsi drinkers did not like the taste, or they did not like the cost of Coca-Cola in their respective towns.

(Believe it or not, soda cost can fluctuate in different areas thanks to simple supply and demand pricing economics.)

So they kicked them out of the room.

What they found with the room full of Coca-Cola drinkers is that if they packaged the product bigger, they would sell more. People drink 12 oz. cans as fast as 8 oz. cans.

They drink 21 oz. bottles as fast as 12 oz. bottles. They drink two liters as fast as one liter. It was a small change that yielded big results.

**Metaphor Points of Construction**

1. Change a client's personal reference to a character in the story.
    A. Client's reference to Coca-Cola
2. Pace the client's situation by linking behaviors and events be-tween the characters in the story and the client's situation.
    A. Coca-Cola trying to increase sales
    B. Direct Connect
        i. Bring the story full circle and explain how the current strategy needs to increase brainstorming for ideas.
3. Find resources for the client within the context of the story.
    A. Coca-Cola's marketing strategy
4. Make sure the story features events in which the characters in the story resolve the conflict and achieve the desired outcome.
    A. Increase in sales

**Pre-Steps**

1. Identify behavior and events
    A. Creativity, small change = big results
2. Strategy in question
    A. Creativity
3. Desired outcomes
    A. New strategies, increased sales
1. Mapping Strategies

**Mapping Strategies**

1. Displace referential characters.

   A. Establish characters (e.g., Coca-Cola, etc.)
   B. Preserve relationship
2. Establish a connection between the client's current situation or behavior and the characters' situations or behaviors.
3. Establish resources of the characters and events.
   A. Strategy, small change = big results
4. Resolution
   A. Ambiguous
      i. Leave it the way the story reads now.
   B. Direct Connect
      i. Bring the story full circle and explain how the current strategy needs to be revamped to brainstorm for ideas.

# Inflation

Back in my early twenties, when I was a financial advisor, I used to live with my 90-year-old granny and take care of her. Every Sunday was our big day out, when I would take Granny to church and then to breakfast.

To prepare for her big day out, Granny would do up her hair, put on the brightest red lipstick and grab the biggest purse ever made. Once we got to the diner it was almost impossible to get Granny to order. Everything was just too expensive!

After much badgering and convincing and assuring Granny that I was paying, she would finally order. That's when I would see clearly why she brought the big purse.

If it was on the table and not nailed down, she was snatching it so she could get her money's worth. Everything went into her purse: all the cream, all the sugar, all the salt and all the pepper. Literally everything went in.

See, Granny grew up during the Great Depression and those were some rough times. Since that traumatic time she has made a habit of living on the bare minimum.

While we can all agree things have gotten a bit better since the Great Depression, prices have consistently risen throughout her lifetime. Inflation has been a big problem in making her money last through the rest of her life.

Even since the invention of Matt Linklater in 1977, prices have risen dramatically.

| Item | 1977 Cost of Living | 2007/08 Cost of Living |
|---|---|---|
| New house | $49,319 | $288,514 |
| New car | $4,785 | $22,000 |
| Tuition to Harvard | $4,100 per year | $31,456 |
| Movie ticket | $2 each | $7.88 each |
| Gallon of gasoline | 65 cents | $3.29 |
| Postage stamp | 13 cents each | 42 cents each |
| Gallon of milk | $1.67 | $3.13 |

*(Facts taken from "Remember When." Find "Remember When" at your local Bob Evans, Cracker Barrel, or http://www.seekpublishing.com/rememberwhen.html)*

**Metaphor Points of Construction**

1. Change a client's personal reference to a character in the story.
   A. Client's reference to Granny
2. Pace the client's situation by linking behaviors and events be-tween the characters in the story and the client's situation.
   A. Granny, their clients or their own behavior
3. Find resources for the client within the context of the story.
   A. Granny and the rising cost of commerce
4. Make sure the story features events in which the characters in the story resolve the conflict and achieve the desired outcome.
   A. Help realize the effects of inflation

## Pre-Steps

1. Identify behavior and events
    A. Why we have to be cautious of inflation, the silent money thief
2. Strategy in question
    A. Not paying attention as inflation eats our money
3. Desired outcomes
    A. Saving more for the future

## Mapping Strategies

1. Displace referential characters.
    A. Establish characters (e.g., Granny, etc.)
    B. Preserve relationship
2. Establish a connection between the client's current situation or behavior and the characters' situations or behaviors.
3. Establish resources of the characters and events.
    A. Rising prices and their effects on people
4. Resolution
    A. Ambiguous
        i. Leave it the way the story reads now.
    B. Direct Connect
        i. Bring the story full circle and explain how the current strategy needs to be revamped to explore saving for the future.

# Driving

I have been driving for about 16 years, and during my illustrious driving career I have totaled four cars.

Three of those happened during my outside sales career.

With that kind of driving record, one would think that I would be petrified to step foot into a car, let alone behind the wheel, and if I were you, I would not step into a vehicle with me – it would be wiser to drive your own car.

Needless to say, I have no choice but to get behind the wheel no matter how reluctant, as I have numerous reasons to build up the courage and stay strong behind the wheel. I need to get to work, go to the grocery store, to family events, etc.

In order for me to feel safe behind the wheel, I do a lot of research to find which vehicle has the best safety ratings.

I need every safety feature known to man to be on that car. Some people look for performance and engine size, but I look for safety ratings, seatbelts and airbags.

As a matter of fact, I will pay extra if they can get me a roll bar, racing seat belts and foam exploding stabilizing airbags.

(I am not sure if car companies actually make those, but for my sake they should.)

In the end, I always settle on a reliable car to get me from point A to point B in the safest manner possible.

I am sure we can all agree that quality and safety is the most important feature to protect our loved ones and ourselves.

## Metaphor Points of Construction

1. Change a client's personal reference to a character in the story.
   A. Me
2. Pace the client's situation by linking behaviors and events between the characters in the story and the client's situation.
   A. Me and my driving career
3. Find resources for the client within the context of the story.
   A. A. Me and my driving career
4. Make sure the story features events in which the characters in the story resolve the conflict and achieve the desired outcome.
   A. Safety and quality

## Pre-Steps

1. Identify behavior and events
   A. Need for safety and quality
2. Strategy in question
   A. Not examining quality and safety
3. Desired outcomes
   A. Buying based on quality and safety

## Mapping Strategies

1. Displace referential characters.
   A. Establish characters (e.g., myself, etc.)
   B. Preserve relationship
2. Establish a connection between the client's current situation or behavior and the characters' situations or behaviors.
3. Establish resources of the characters and events.
   A. Buying quality and safety

4. Resolution
    A. Ambiguous
        i. Leave it the way the story reads now.
    B. Direct Connect
        i. Bring the story full circle to explain how the current strategy needs to be revamped to ensure quality and safety are at the forefront.

# Suit Story

Think about the day you went shopping for your first suit, or the first time you splurged on an expensive suit. Undoubtedly you were nervous about what you should buy, how much you might spend or how you would look.

The one thing that can make you feel more comfortable about your decision is a professional, knowledgeable suit salesman. The salesman will make you try on a few different cuts and styles until you find the one that looks the best on you.

The salesman will build up your confidence by telling you how the suit is the perfect cut, size and fit for you. With all the attention to detail, you may even feel like you are buying something as intricate as a diamond.

At this point, any feelings of nervousness are long gone and you have begun to visualize your impending new success.

In the end you will often envision how great you will look at an upcoming event, or how much money you will make wearing this suit.

What you spend no longer matters, because you know this suit is the right one for you. How can you transfer this to your clients, getting them to try on your product and visualize the success they will have with its utilization?

**Metaphor Points of Construction**

1. Change a client's personal reference to a character in the story.
   A. Client's reference to a suit buying experience

2. Pace the client's situation by linking behaviors and events between the characters in the story and the client's situation.
    A. Relate them to the salesmen, their clients to me
3. Find resources for the client within the context of the story.
    A. Relate them to the salesmen, their clients to me
4. Make sure the story features events in which the characters in the story resolve the conflict and achieve the desired outcome.
    A. How to get a client to 'try on' your product

**Pre-Steps**

1. Identify behavior and events
    A. Help the client visualize success
2. Strategy in question
    A. Not getting clients to visualize success
3. Desired outcomes
    A. Getting the client to better visualize success

**Mapping Strategies**

1. Displace referential characters.
    A. Establish characters (e.g., the salesman and client)
    B. Preserve relationship
2. Establish a connection between the client's current situation or behavior and the characters' situations or behaviors.
3. Establish resources of the characters and events.
    A. Salesman, client, visualization
4. Resolution

A. Ambiguous
    i. Leave it the way the story reads now.
B. Direct Connect
    i. Bring the story full circle and explain how the current strategy needs to be revamped to get the client to visualize success with your product.

# Pig and the Python

For those of you who like nature shows, you have undoubtedly seen images of a python trying to eat a wild pig.

At first you cannot believe the python will even get a bite out of the pig, but the next thing you know, the pig is swallowed whole and the only sign it even existed is that big bulge slithering down the python's belly.

Back in the 1950s, a similar scenario happened in America. Think of the python as the US economy and the pig as the Baby Boom generation. As the Baby Boom generation started, our economy had to get its jaws around a big pig.

This huge boom seemed daunting at first, but eventually the python stretched its jaws wide and got the pig into its mouth. Swallowing such a large pig created great opportunities for the economy. Below you'll see examples of these opportunities in each time period.

- 1940s/50s: As Boomers are being born and raised, there is a huge need for products to help housewives such as disposable diapers and pre-packaged baby food (think Gerber).
- 1960s/70s: As Boomers come of age, they develop their own tastes and begin to cut loose. Discos start to pop up on every corner and go-go boots become popular.
- 1980s: As Boomers leave the family home, then get tired of paying rent, the American economy sees a tremendous real estate boom as they purchase their first homes.

- 1990s/2000s: As Boomers get older they begin to invest. We see a tremendous period of growth in the stock market and major advances made in technology.
- 2010-and beyond: As Boomers prepare for retirement... (to be continued)

In every time period we see an entire industry revolutionized by the Boomers.

The pig always seems too big to pass through the python, but the economy has been able to swallow the pig whole every time.

As we approach this age of Baby Boomer retirement, it is clear that we stand to see huge change and growth in different areas of our economy.

**Metaphor Points of Construction**

1. Change a client's personal reference to a character in the story.
   A. Target reference to how they can capitalize from the Baby Boomers
2. Pace the client's situation by linking behaviors and events be-tween the characters in the story and the client's situation.
   A. The different products that had success due to the huge consumer base of the Boomers.
3. Find resources for the client within the context of the story.
   A. Their products and how they can capitalize

4. Make sure the story features events in which the characters in the story resolve the conflict and achieve the desired outcome.
    A. How to fit their product into the consumer base

**Pre-Steps**

1. Identify behavior and events
    A. Strategize how to meet the demands of Baby Boomers.
2. Strategy in question
    A. Not effectively targeting Baby Boomers
3. Desired outcomes
    A. Get the audience to realize the mass consumer base that boomers represent.

**Mapping Strategies**

1. Displace referential characters.
    A. Establish characters (e.g., Boomers, etc.)
    B. Preserve relationship
2. Establish a connection between the client's current situation or behavior and the characters' situations or behaviors.
3. Establish resources of the characters and events
    A. Boomers = consumers; our products = next big boom
4. Resolution
    A. Ambiguous
        i. Leave it the way the story reads now.
    B. Direct Connect
        i. Bring the story full circle to explain how the current strategy needs to be revamped to get the client to

visualize success by targeting Boomers.

# The Soap Story

I want you to envision a bar of soap. Imagine washing your hands repeatedly over a long period of time. We can all agree that every time we wash our hands, the bar of soap will slowly start to wither away. Now I want you to imagine that you have an Uncle Sam (that is, if you already do not). Think of Uncle Sam also washing his hands with the bar of soap. We can all agree that another set of hands on our soap will only make it wither away faster. Now, I want you to replace the bar of soap with your money. As with the soap, the more hands that touch our money, the quicker it withers away. The key is to put the soap (or your money) in a safe place with the least amount of hands on it.

**Metaphor Points of Construction**

1. Change a client's personal reference to a character in the story.
    A. Link the audience and their money to the soap and its utilization
2. Pace the client's situation by linking behaviors and events between the characters in the story and the client's situation.
    A. How frequent, frivolous use of the soap will lead to it withering away
3. Find resources for the client within the context of the story.
    A. How similar, careless use of their money will result in it withering away
4. Make sure the story features events in which the characters in the story resolve the conflict and achieve the desired outcome.

   A. How to properly take care of their money

**Pre-Steps**

1. Identify behavior and events
   A. Protecting their money
2. Strategy in question
   A. Spending money frivolously
3. Desired outcomes
   A. Get the audience to realize the safe keeping of money can make it last.

**Mapping Strategies**

1. Displace referential characters
   A. Establish characters (e.g., the soap users, etc.)
   B. Preserve relationship
2. Establish a connection between the client's current situation or behavior and the characters' situations or behaviors.
3. Establish resources of the characters and events
   A. Soap users = the audience; soap= their money
4. Resolution
   A. Ambiguous
      i. Leave it the way the story reads now.
   B. Direct Connect
      i. Bring the story full circle to explain how the current strategy needs to be revamped in order to have better strategies for money management, so it does not wither away like the bar of soap.

# Nighttime Ritual

What is your nighttime ritual? We all have one.

Some of us may sit down with a glass of wine. Some of us may sit down with a beer.

Some of us may sit down with a cup of tea to unwind. Others, well, maybe that's personal.

But I bet for the majority of us, our nighttime ritual involves watching the evening news.

What channel do you watch and why?

I have moved to four different markets in the past eight years, and each time I am faced with the daunting task of finding my favorite local sportscaster.

Five years ago, I moved back to Chicago and I tried out all the local networks: WGN, ABC, NBC and CBS.

In the end I settled on a guy named Mark Giangreco from ABC-7. What I liked about him was that while the sports stories were all the same, his delivery of the stories was always different.

Mark had the best and most dynamic way of delivering the sports, thanks to upbeat nicknames and clever euphemisms.

The sales industry is exactly the same. All the salespeople are similar people with very similar stories working towards a similar goal.

So in the end, the question is, "What makes your story unique?"

How do you tell your story with an undeniable charisma?

How do you differentiate yourself?

## Metaphor Points of Construction

1. Change a client's personal reference to a character in the story.
   A. Audience = sportscaster
2. Pace the client's situation by linking behaviors and events be-tween the characters in the story and the client's situation.
   A. Audience = Sportscaster
3. Find resources for the client within the context of the story.
   A. Audience story = Sportscaster story
4. Make sure the story features events in which the characters in the story resolve the conflict and achieve the desired outcome.
   A. Be as dynamic as a sportscaster.

## Pre-Steps

1. Identify behavior and events
   A. Not being as dynamic or memorable as they could be
2. Strategy in question
   A. Being more dynamic in client interface
3. Desired outcomes
   A. Being more dynamic

## Mapping Strategies

1. Displace referential characters
   A. Establish Characters (e.g., sportscaster, etc.)
   B. Preserve Relationship
2. Establish a connection between the client's current situation or behavior, and the characters' situations or behaviors.
3. Establish resources of the characters and events.
   A. Sportscaster = Success = Dynamic
   B. Audience = Success = Dynamic

4. Resolution
    A. Ambiguous
        i. Leave it the way the story reads now.
    B. Direct Connect
        i. Bring the story full circle, illustrating ways that an audience can increase their likeability.

# Limited by Materials

I want to share a story about someone who has been in my life for the past 31 years, my brother Todd.

Todd is a pitching coach for the Flyers, a Division 1 baseball team at the University of Dayton in Dayton, Ohio.

During his decade as a college baseball coach, Todd has put 16 pitchers into the pros, versus zero position players. You're probably thinking, "That's what he's supposed to do." I agree with you.

In addition, his pitching staff is continuously one of the top pitching staffs in the Atlantic Ten Conference.

Again you're thinking, "That's what he's supposed to do." I agree with you.

In 2008, his staff was ranked 30th out 286 Division 1 pitching staffs. Again, you're thinking, "That's what he's supposed to do." I agree with you.

The thing that is truly impressive about my brother's track record is that he's achieved these remarkable numbers despite many obstacles. First of all, Todd coaches at a Midwestern school, where it's not easy to recruit top talent to a cold weather state for a warm weather sport.

Additionally, the program is under-funded. The Flyers are only allocated eight scholarships per year, compared to the maximum of 11.7 scholarships for other Division 1 programs.

The moral of the story is that Todd could use all these obstacles as excuses, but instead he chooses to be a success.

The same applies to our industry. We can always make the excuses that our product is not good enough, or that we do not have the right tools.

But at the end of the day it is truly up to us to decide if we want to be successful. You don't just become suddenly successful. You have to work at being successful every day of your life. Are you on the cause side of the cause and effect equation, or the effect side? Be the cause for everything in your life.

### Metaphor Points of Construction

1. Change a client's personal reference to a character in the story.
   A. Audience = Todd
2. Pace the client's situation by linking behaviors and events between the characters in the story and the client's situation.
   A. Audience = Todd
3. Find resources for the client within the context of the story.
   A. Audience's situation = Todd's story
4. Make sure the story features events in which the characters in the story resolve the conflict and achieve the desired outcome.
   A. The audience can have success just like Todd.

### Pre-Steps

1. Identify behavior and events
   A. Excuses
2. Strategy in question
   A. Not being on the cause side of the cause and effect equation

3. Desired outcomes
    A. Be on the cause side

**Mapping Strategies**

1. Displace referential characters
    A. Establish characters (e.g., the audience as Todd, etc.)
    B. Preserve relationship
2. Establish a connection between the client's current situation or behavior, and the characters' situations or behaviors.
3. Establish resources of the characters and events.
    A. Audience = Todd
    B. Cause vs. effect
4. Resolution
    A. Ambiguous
        i. Leave it the way the story reads now.
    B. Direct Connect
        i. Explain that excuses are inexcusable.

# Vince Lombardi

For those of you who do not know Vince Lombardi, he coached the Green Bay Packers from 1959 to 1967. He is arguably the greatest football coach of all time, winning five League Championships and two Super Bowls during his tenure.

Lombardi prided himself on being a guy who believed in the basics. He would start every pre-season camp by holding up a football and saying, "Gentlemen, this is a football!"

The point is, Lombardi believed that focusing on fundamentals was what separated the good from the great. The same holds true in business. Great and successful people are separated from the average not by working harder, but by executing the fundamentals flawlessly.

**Metaphor Points of Construction**

1. Change a client's personal reference to a character in the story.
    A. Audience = Lombardi's Green Bay Packers
2. Pace the client's situation by linking behaviors and events be-tween the characters in the story and the client's situation.
    A. Audience = Lombardi's Green Bay Packers
3. Find resources for the client within the context of the story.
    A. Execute the fundamentals
4. Make sure the story features events in which the characters in the story resolve the conflict and achieve the desired outcome.

A. Focus on fundamentals

**Pre-Steps**

1. Identify behavior and events
   A. Not practicing correct fundamentals
2. Strategy in question
   A. The basics
3. Desired outcomes
   A. Becoming more fundamentally sound

**Mapping Strategies**

1. Displace referential characters
   A. Establish characters (e.g., Lombardi's team, etc.)
   B. Preserve relationship
2. Establish a connection between the client's current situation or behavior, and the characters' situations or behaviors.
3. Establish resources of the characters and events
   A. Audience = Lombardi's team
   B. Audience = Fundamentals = Success
4. Resolution
   A. Ambiguous
      i. Leave it the way the story reads now.
   B. Direct Connect
      i. Bring the story full circle to explain ways that the audience can improve upon fundamentals.

# The Golden Bear

Jack Nicklaus is widely regarded as the greatest golfer of all time. In his 25-year career, he accumulated a record 18 professional major wins, and in addition, he won eight majors on the senior tour.

Several years ago, Jack was asked by the King of Saudi Arabia to come play golf. After declining many invitations, Jack finally said yes.

The King sent his private jet to the states to fly Jack over to Saudi Arabia, where he stayed with the King for a week. They spent each day playing 36 holes of golf. During the week Jack ate and lived, well, like a king.

At the end of the week, the King asked him, "Jack, you came and played golf with me. I greatly appreciate you taking the time. Is there anything in the world that I can possibly do for you?"

As all of us would do, Jack declined. He said, "I couldn't possibly. We played golf. I ate and drank like a king. There is nothing I could possibly ask for." The King persisted.

Finally, Jack said, "You know what? I collect golf clubs. Buy me a golf club." The King replied, "Great!"

On the way back to the United States, Jack was again on the King's private plane. The King's jet was gaudier than anything that Donald Trump could even imagine, decked out in gold and jewels.

Jack started to fantasize about the golf club that the King would send him. He thought it might be diamond-encrusted, jewel-encrusted or possibly solid gold.

Jack returned home, a few months passed, and he had forgotten about the golf club. But after three months, Jack received a certified letter in the mail from the King. He opened up the letter and inside was a deed for a 500-acre golf club.

The moral of the story is that the King thinks bigger than Jack. Jack was thinking a golf club and the king was thinking a GOLF CLUB.

THINK BIG!

## Metaphor Points of Construction

1. Change a client's personal reference to a character in the story.
    A. Audience = Jack Nicklaus
2. Pace the client's situation by linking behaviors and events be-tween the characters in the story and the client's situation.
    A. Audience = Jack Nicklaus
3. Find resources for the client within the context of the story.
    A. Audience's frame of mind = Jack Nicklaus' frame of mind
4. Make sure the story features events in which the characters in the story resolve the conflict and achieve the desired outcome.
    A. Think big!

## Pre-Steps

1. Identify behavior and events
    A. Not thinking as big as possible

A. Strategy in question
    a. Think bigger
B. Desired outcomes
    a. Make a habit of thinking big.

**Mapping Strategies**

1. Displace referential characters.
    A. Establish characters (e.g., Jack Nicklaus, etc.)
    B. Preserve relationship
2. Establish a connection between the client's current situation or behavior and the characters' situations or behaviors.
3. Establish resources of the characters and events
    A. King of Saudi Arabia = Think big
    B. Audience = Think big
4. Resolution
    A. Ambiguous
        i. Leave it the way the story reads now.
    B. Direct Connect
        i. Bring the story full circle, offering the audience examples of how they can think bigger.

# John Wooden

Who is wearing socks? I would venture a guess that most of you are. If you're like me, you just throw on a pair and run out the door – hopefully accompanied by a pair of shoes. But why do I ask?

In the early sixties, there was a college basketball coach that began each season with an entire practice devoted to teaching his players how to put on their socks.

That's right, the first day of practice was not spent playing defense, shooting free throws or learning how to full-court press. Whether you were a freshman or senior, you were taught how to put on your socks.

His process was as follows:

- Place your toe in a fully-rolled sock and align your toes with the seam.
- Begin to roll the sock down your foot, smoothing it out as you go.
- Pull the sock over your heel while not allowing it to bunch.
- Finish by pulling the sock as high as it goes. (Remember, there was only one type of athletic sock in the 1960s.)

Once you knew how to put on your socks, the coach would then tell you your shoe size. He did not care what size shoe you thought you were.

See, most kids are taught to buy shoes with room for growth, but once those shoes actually fit, they're worn out and it's time for a new pair.

Thus, most people don't know what a proper fitting shoe feels like. So why pay such close attention to shoes and socks?

It seems that in the 1960s, the number one reason for players to take time off was blisters, which were most commonly caused by improperly fitting socks and shoes.

This coach's philosophy was that in order to succeed he needed his best players on the floor, and he was determined to protect his players from themselves. Instituting such rigid processes would achieve this. Though seemingly crazy and extreme, his process produced the following results:

- 10 NCAA Championships, seven of which were consecutive
- 885 career wins
- Multiple players and coaches inducted into the NBA Hall of Fame
- The title of the greatest basketball coach in NCAA history

That coach was John Wooden, and his process became known as the John Wooden "Game Plan for Life." Wooden's philosophy was that the things within a person's control - such as attention to detail and dedication to hard work - are more important than the talents with which someone is born.

The point is, in both good and bad times, it's imperative that you stay focused on the basics. We all have systems in place that help us do our jobs better, but it's easy to drift away. Wooden never drifted from his "Game Plan for Life," and it's obvious his dedication to the little things paid off in a big way.

Stay focused on the basics and do them to the best of your ability.

## Metaphor Points of Construction

1. Change a client's personal reference to a character in the story.
    A. Audience = Wooden and his team
2. Pace the client's situation by linking behaviors and events be-tween the characters in the story and the client's situation.
    A. Audience = Wooden and his team
3. Find resources for the client within the context of the story.
    A. Audience's story = Wooden's story
4. Make sure the story features events in which the characters in the story resolve the conflict and achieve the desired outcome.
    A. Focus on the basics

## Pre-Steps

1. Identify behavior and events
    A. Not paying attention to the small things
2. Strategy in question
    A. Become more disciplined
3. Desired outcomes
    A. Being more disciplined with the basics

## Mapping Strategies

1. Displace referential characters
    A. Establish characters (e.g., Wooden's team, etc.)
    B. Preserve relationship

2. Establish a connection between the client's current situation or behavior and the characters' situations or behaviors.
3. Establish resources of the characters and events.
    A. Wooden's team = Discipline
    B. Audience = Success = Discipline
4. Resolution
    A. Ambiguous
        i. Leave it the way the story reads now.
    B. Direct Connect
        i. Bring the story full circle to demonstrate ways that the audience can increase their attention to detail.

# Snorkeling in Rough Waters

A few years ago, I took a four-day trip to South Beach. The weather was fantastic. It was sunny and 80 degrees every day. I had intentions of just relaxing and hanging out by the pool, but one day I decided to plan an excursion, and selected an enjoyable snorkeling trip – or so I thought.

The day started out great. I boarded the boat and had a relaxing ride. The sun was beating down on my face and the wind was in my hair.

Then, the terror began.

The boat stopped and began to rock back and forth so violently that when the right side came up you couldn't see the shore, and when the left side rocked up you couldn't see the horizon. I started to get ill.

To add insult to injury, the skipper happened to be a guy I played football against in college. Not only did he beat me on the field, but now I was getting sick on his boat!

In the end, I was so ill that I couldn't snorkel. I had to just sit on the boat in misery until the expedition was done.

They told me that if I looked at the horizon or the shore, it would help me feel better. This proved not to be 100 percent true.

What really helped was staring at the shore knowing that in just an hour I would be back safely on dry land.

Finally, we arrived back on the shore, eventually my stomach calmed down and I was able to enjoy the rest of the day and the rest of my vacation.

This experience is what most of us face from time to time, whether in business or our personal lives.

We all have goals and aspirations – but we often hit rough waters. Do not focus on the rough patch, but focus on the goal and the horizon.

**Metaphor Points of Construction**

1. Change a client's personal reference to a character in the story.
    A. Audience = My experience
2. Pace the client's situation by linking behaviors and events be-tween the characters in the story and the client's situation.
    A. Audience = My experience
3. Find resources for the client within the context of the story.
    A. Audience's frame of mind = My frame of mind
4. Make sure the story features events in which the characters in the story resolve the conflict and achieve the desired outcome.
    A. Stay focused!

**Pre-Steps**

1. Identify behavior and events
    A. Not staying focused on the big picture
2. Strategy in question
    A. Learning to stay focused
3. Desired outcomes
    A. Goal achievement

**Mapping Strategies**

1. Displace referential characters.
    A. Establish characters (e.g., me)
    B. Preserve relationship

2. Establish a connection between the client's current situation or behavior and the characters' situations or behaviors.
3. Establish resources of the characters and events.
    A. Me = Horizon
    B. Audience = Goal oriented
4. Resolution
    A. Ambiguous
        i. Leave it the way the story reads now.
    B. Direct Connect
        i. Bring the story full circle to show the audience how they can stay focused on clearly defined goals.

## Hit the Slopes

Seven years ago when I lived in New Jersey, I picked up the great sport of skiing. Since then I have been skiing about 20 times, including some great ski trips to Vermont, Lake Tahoe, Mammouth and Breckenridge.

During the first day of my ski trip to Breckenridge, I began to get a little cocky, certain that my youthful athletic prowess was back.

The second day of the trip, I started to take on and conquer black diamonds. I looked like a pro, that is, for most of the day.

On one of my last runs, I ran into some trouble. I was riding the ski lift up, as I had numerous times that day, when half-way up the mountain the adversities set in. My goggles started to fog up. Then, they iced over.

Suddenly, the snow started to come down in sheets. The conditions became so treacherous so quickly, that I could barely exit the chair lift.

Here I was, at the top of a black diamond with no vision, thanks to my iced-over goggles and a blizzard of snow. I started to get nervous and my mind started to play tricks on me.

My legs and body began to tighten. I had no choice but to start down the mountain, visually impaired and beaten up.

Almost as soon as I started down, my skis came out from under me and I flew up, remaining suspended in the air for what seemed like ten minutes. I couldn't see what was happening due to my iced-over goggles.

All of a sudden I landed on the back of my head and neck, then continued to slide to the bottom of the hill.

As I lay there, taking inventory of any damages and contemplating if I had a concussion, another skier slammed into the back of me.

Finally, I peeled my beaten body off the snow, made it cautiously and safely to the bottom, and headed directly to the bar for some hot chocolate and Schnapps.

**Metaphor Points of Construction**

1. Change a client's personal reference to a character in the story.
    A. Audience = Me
2. Pace the client's situation by linking behaviors and events be-tween the characters in the story and the client's situation.
    A. Audience = Me
3. Find resources for the client within the context of the story.
    A. Audience's frame of mind = My frame of mind
4. Make sure the story features events in which the characters in the story resolve the conflict and achieve the desired outcome.
    A. Stay focused

**Pre-Steps**

1. Identify behavior and events
    A. Letting the elements cloud your thinking
2. Strategy in question
    A. Stay focused
3. Desired outcomes
    A. More focus

## Mapping Strategies

1. Displace referential characters.
    - A. Establish characters (e.g., me)
    - B. Preserve relationship
2. Establish a connection between the client's current situation or behavior and the characters' situations or behaviors.
3. Establish resources of the characters and events.
    - A. Me = Not focused
    - B. Audience = Stay focused
4. Resolution
    - A. Ambiguous
        - i. Leave it the way the story reads now.
    - B. Direct Connect
        - i. Bring the story full circle and demonstrate ways the audience can increase their focus on the task at hand.

# Matty Link Learns to Swim

Recently, I was reminded of my days as a kid and my experiences at my local pool, the Lakewood Aqua Club. At the Lakewood Aqua Club, each kid had to pass a swimming test to be able to attend the pool without adult supervision.

This was the goal of every kid in the neighborhood, including me, as I hated having to go with my parents or one of my older brothers.

The test was to be able to swim one length of an Olympic-size pool. This was a daunting task. Not only did the distance seem insurmountable, but also all of my brothers and their buddies would be watching.

I wanted to get across the pool so desperately, but I couldn't go the distance. The lifeguard would be to my right, and I would build up the courage to jump in and start the doggy paddle (not the ideal stroke to make it the length of the pool).

Needless to say, with the doggy paddle stroke I was always unsuccessful. I was using a procedure designed to keep you afloat and essentially stationary.

Finally, after many attempts, I switched to the freestyle stroke. I didn't make it the first couple times, but thankfully, I had the lifeguard nearby to throw me a life preserver or to jump in after me.

Yet each time I made progress, getting a little bit further than I did the last time.

One day I completed the task and made it safely to the other end, and finally, I could attend the pool without any adult supervision. This was my first step into manhood!

**Metaphor Points of Construction**

1. Change a client's personal reference to a character in the story.
    A. Audience = Me
2. Pace the client's situation by linking behaviors and events be-tween the characters in the story and the client's situation.
    A. Audience = Me
3. Find resources for the client within the context of the story.
    A. Audience taking chances = My own risk-taking
4. Make sure the story features events in which the characters in the story resolve the conflict and achieve the desired outcome.
    A. Take chances

**Pre-Steps**

1. Identify behavior and events
    A. Not taking chances
2. Strategy in question
    A. Learning to take chances
3. Desired outcomes
    A. Make a habit of taking chances

**Mapping Strategies**

1. Displace referential characters.
    A. Establish characters (e.g., me)
    B. Preserve relationship

2. Establish a connection between the client's current situation or behavior and the characters' situations and behaviors.
3. Establish resources of the characters and events.
    - A. Me = Take chances = Success
    - B. Audience = Take chances = Success
4. Resolution
    - A. Ambiguous
        - i. Leave it the way the story reads now.
    - B. Direct Connect
        - i. Bring the story full circle and explain the ways the audience can take more calculated chances.

## Selling Features Before Benefits

Once again, I would like to bring up my illustrious driving career. Remember how I have totaled four cars in the past 15 years? Well here's a story about when I had some car trouble, and how features and benefits tied into the sales process of buying a new car.

I had just moved to New Jersey from Pittsburgh, Pennsylvania. A month into my new journey, I totaled my Nissan Altima.

I was driving into Delaware early in the morning, approaching a light that had just turned from red to green. I started coasting and looked down briefly at my directions, when out of nowhere I smashed into the back of a pick-up truck. The airbag slammed into my chest, and it was obvious the car was totaled.

After we exchanged insurance information, I got myself together, went to the local Enterprise to rent a car and carried out my appointments for the rest of the day.

Obviously I needed a new car, and I decided on a used Nissan Maxima. I walked into the first dealership and was approached by an excited salesperson. He shook my hand and asked me what I was in the market for. I told him a Nissan Maxima.

He rushed me over to a brand new Nissan Maxima, then bent down and pointed to the tire. He said, "17-inch aluminum alloy-rimmed wheels!" I don't know about you, but I had no clue what that meant.

Next, he sat me down in the leather driver's seat. But I wasn't a fan.

As my mom always points out, leather is hot in the summer and cold in the winter.

Then he startled me and pushed a button on the seat, igniting the seat warmer. It was November 1st, 60 degrees outside, and this guy is trying to make my butt warm. I was a bit puzzled.

Next, he showed me how to control the radio from the steering wheel. But I don't listen to the radio in the car, as I am always on the phone. In addition, the car was brand new.

Do you know how much a Nissan Maxima costs? I have never paid more than $15,000 for a car, and I wasn't about to start at that moment. I bolted out of the dealership.

I truly just wanted to go home, but I still needed a car, so I visited another dealership. Yet again, another salesman approached me. He asked me to sit down in his office and proceeded to ask me questions for about 30 minutes. I started to get a little antsy.

"Perfect," he finally said, and led me to the showroom. The salesman brought me to a used Nissan Maxima for $15,000. He got down on his knee and said, "17-inch aluminum alloy-rimmed wheels. Do you know what that means to you, Matt?"

I shrugged my shoulders. He explained that 17s have more surface area then my old 16-inch wheels; that more surface area means I might have been able to stop before I smashed into the back of the pick-up truck.

Next, he sat me on the leather seat. He exclaimed, "I know, I know! Your mom always said that leather was hot in the summer and cold in the winter."

He then excused himself as he pushed the button near my butt. He explained, "Your seat is about to heat up. I know that may not mean much on a day like today, but in January when you are going in and out of those sales calls all day, you'll appreciate a warm seat."

He then put my hands on the wheel and showed me where I could control the radio. He said, "I know you probably don't listen to the radio, but I can almost bet the day you got into your accident you were on the phone, looking at your directions, eating an Egg McMuffin and leaning over playing with the radio. Now, instead of reaching over you can change the radio station right in front of you." I was sold!

Rather than speaking generally, which was like a foreign language to me, the second salesman showed me how all the features of the car benefited my life and would keep me safe.

The point is that we need to make sure we focus on the features when selling our product as well.

**Metaphor Points of Construction**

1. Change a client's personal reference to a character in the story.
   A. Audience = Salespeople
2. Pace the client's situation by linking behaviors and events between the characters in the story and the client's situation.
   A. Audience = My experience
3. Find resources for the client within the context of the story.
   A. Audience's sales approach = Car salesmen's strategy

4. Make sure the story features events in which the characters in the story resolve the conflict and achieve the desired outcome.
    A. Tying benefits to needs

**Pre-Steps**

1. Identify behavior and events
    A. Selling strategies
2. Strategy in question
    A. Not selling based on features
3. Desired outcomes
    A. Selling benefits

**Mapping Strategies**

1. Displace referential characters
    A. Establish characters (e.g., the car salesman, etc.)
    B. Preserve relationship
2. Establish a connection between the client's current situation or behavior and the characters' situations or behaviors.
3. Establish resources of the characters and events.
    A. Car salesmen selling benefits
    B. Audience selling benefits
4. Resolution
    A. Ambiguous
        i. Leave it the way the story reads now.
    B. Direct Connect
        i. Bring the story full circle to demonstrate ways the audience can sell their products more successfully.

# Wonder Woman

Sometimes, when reps get the tough questions on how someone or something can help, they may freeze up. So allow me to draw a parallel for you using one of my favorite super heroes: Wonder Woman!

Do any of you remember Wonder Woman? She had the Golden Lasso to rope in perpetrators; she had the Golden Cuffs to deflect the bullets.

Every day we get bullets shot at each of us, just like Wonder Woman. The bullets are the hard questions or objections that you do not know the answers to when trying to keep a client happy, or trying to sell a prospective customer.

What I want to do is supply you with some scripted answers, or Golden Cuffs, to deflect those questions or objections, whether they are simple or serious.

**Metaphor Points of Construction**

1. Change a client's personal reference to a character in the story.
   A. Audience = Wonder Woman
2. Pace the client's situation by linking behaviors and events be-tween the characters in the story and the client's situation.
   A. Audience = Wonder Woman
3. Find resources for the client within the context of the story.
   A. Audience's experience = Wonder Woman's experience

4. Make sure the story features events in which the characters in the story resolve the conflict and achieve the desired outcome.
    A. Overcoming objections

**Pre-Steps**

1. Identify behavior and events
    A. Having the perfect response to questions or objections
2. Strategy in question
    A. Not having answers to questions or objections
3. Desired outcomes
    A. Scripted responses

**Mapping Strategies**

1. Displace referential characters.
    A. Establish characters (e.g., Wonder Woman, etc.)
    B. Preserve relationship
2. Establish a connection between the client's current situation or behavior and the characters' situations or behaviors.
3. Establish resources of the characters and events
    A. Wonder Woman = Gold Cuffs
    B. Audience = Scripted responses
4. Resolution
    A. Ambiguous
        i. Leave it the way the story reads now.
    B. Direct Connect
        i. Bring the story full circle and offer scripted responses for the audience.

# The Best Referrer

Surprisingly, the greatest referrer I had when I was an advisor at Olde Discount was my granny. During your first 30 days at Olde, you had to get your Series 52 license, which allowed you to sell bonds and most fixed-income investments.

During your first 90 days, you had to sell $250,000 to be able to move on and take your Series 7 license exam. When I got to this point at Olde, I had a week to go before I took my 7 or I was fired.

During a casual conversation one evening, I mentioned to my granny that we had 7 percent CDs in inventory at work. Granny was so excited that she invested $10,000, and in her true 90-year-old fashion, she told all her friends in the neighborhood about the great thing that I did for her.

Later that same night, all of Granny's friends were over at the house inquiring about the great CDs that I could offer. Needless to say, I was not fired, and I more than surpassed my goal. The reason I am telling you this is because I realize that not everyone has a great granny like mine, and we all need another way to get referrals.

Here are two options:

**Number 1: The lost art of sending thank you cards**

Sending a thank you note is a simple task, something you can even do while watching "American Idol."

The card should read something like this: "Thank you for allowing me to be a part of your company's / family's X business. If you have any friends / colleagues who also need help with their X business, feel free to hand out my card." (Of course, enclose some cards.)

The great thing about writing a thank you note is that it's non-invasive, and you can send it during any point of the sales process.

**Number 2: Craft a story**

Often it helps to tell a story or anecdote to a client to illustrate the way in which you can be an asset to them or their business.

Here's an example of a quick but effective anecdote that can yield a positive referral:

Recently I was sitting in front of a client who came to me with problem X. They were about to make decision X for problem X, and it was clearly the wrong decision for them.

I helped them make the right decision. But what occurred to me is that many people or businesses may be making the same wrong decision. Do you know anyone who may be going down that path? I would love to help them make the right decision.

**Metaphor Points of Construction**

1. Change a client's personal reference to a character in the story.
    A. Audience = Me
2. Pace the client's situation by linking behaviors and events between the characters in the story and the client's situation.
    A. Audience = Me
3. Find resources for the client within the context of the story.
    A. Audience's referral process = My own process

4. Make sure the story features events in which the characters in the story resolve the conflict and achieve the desired outcome.
    A. Ask for referrals

**Pre-Steps**

1. Identify behavior and events
    A. Not asking for referrals
2. Strategy in question
    A. Referral process
3. Desired outcomes
    A. More referrals

**Mapping Strategies**

1. Displace referential characters.
    A. Establish characters (e.g., me)
    B. Preserve relationship
2. Establish a connection between the client's current situation or behavior and the characters' situations or behaviors.
3. Establish resources of the characters and events.
    A. Me = Referral process
    B. Audience = Implement a process
4. Resolution
    B. Ambiguous
        i. Leave it the way the story reads now.
    C. Direct Connect
        i. Bring the story full circle and explain ways that the audience can ask for referrals.

# Waiter/Waitress

Do you think a waiter or waitress is a salesperson? Absolutely!

Tips make up a large portion of their pay every single night. Tips are definitely an incentive for the waiter or waitress to give great service.

Recently, when I was dining in a restaurant in Chicago, the waitress handed over the check and asked, "You wouldn't want anything else, would ya?"

Not only was this improper English, but it was also a poor way to sell me on ordering dessert. The right way would have been for the waitress to bring out a tray of desserts to get my mouth watering, and to explain to me which one is her favorite and why.

At that point, it's almost impossible to pass up a sweet treat, but the waitress's poor sales techniques kept me from asking for the dessert menu. At the end of the day, what did that mean to the waitress? Since a dessert can be about 10 to 20 percent of the bill, if I am willing to buy some chocolate cake, her tip would only go up.

By using better sales techniques, the waitress could make more money and be successful. In the end, a great sale will always boil down to not only what you say, but also how you say it.

**Metaphor Points of Construction**

1. Change a client's personal reference to a character in the story.
    A. Audience = Waitress

2. Pace the client's situation by linking behaviors and events be-tween the characters in the story and the client's situation.
    A. Audience = Waitress
3. Find resources for the client within the context of the story.
    A. Audience's sales techniques = Waitress's sales techniques
4. Make sure the story features events in which the characters in the story resolve the conflict and achieve the desired outcome.
    A. Better sales techniques

**Pre-Steps**

1. Identify behavior and events
    A. Not saying the right thing for the best outcome
2. Strategy in question
    A. Sales techniques
3. Desired outcomes
    A. Thinking up better ways to sell

**Mapping Strategies**

1. Displace referential characters.
    A. Establish characters (e.g., the waitress, etc.)
    B. Preserve relationship
2. Establish a connection between the client's current situation or behavior and the characters' situations or behaviors.
3. Establish resources of the characters and events
    A. Waitress = Bad techniques
    B. Audience = Better techniques
4. Resolution

A. Ambiguous
    i. Leave it the way the story reads now
B. Direct Connect
    i. Bring the story full circle to demonstrate ways that the audience can establish better selling techniques.

# The Lady in the Gingham Dress

This story begins with a lady in a faded gingham dress and her husband, dressed in a dingy suit, stepping off a train in Boston, and trying to get into the president of Harvard's office without an appointment.

The president's secretary could tell instantly that such backwoods, country hicks had no business at Harvard and probably didn't even deserve to be in Cambridge.

"We want to see the president," the man said softly. "He'll be busy all day," the secretary snapped. "We'll wait," said the lady.

For hours the secretary ignored them, hoping that the couple would finally become discouraged and go away. But they didn't.

The secretary grew frustrated and finally decided to disturb the president. "Maybe if they just see you for a few minutes, they'll finally leave," she told him. He sighed in exasperation and nodded. Someone of his importance obviously didn't have time to waste with these visitors.

Looking stern, the president strutted toward the couple. The lady told him, "We had a son that attended Harvard for one year. He loved Harvard. He was happy here. But about a year ago, he was accidentally killed. My husband and I would like to erect a memorial to him somewhere on campus."

The president wasn't touched – he was shocked. "Madam," he said gruffly. "We cannot put up a statue for every person who attended Harvard and died. If we did, this place would look like a cemetery."

"Oh no," the lady explained. "We don't want to erect a statue. We would like to give a building to Harvard."

The president rolled his eyes. He glanced at the gingham dress and homespun suit, and then exclaimed, "A building? Do you have any earthly idea how much a building costs? We have over seven and a half million dollars in physical property at Harvard."

For a moment, the lady was silent. The president was pleased; he could get rid of them now.

The lady turned to her husband and said quietly, "Is that all it costs to start a university? Why don't we just start our own?" Her husband nodded. The president's face wilted in confusion and bewilderment.

Mr. and Mrs. Leland Stanford walked away and traveled to Palo Alto, California, where they established the university that bears their name, a memorial to a son that Harvard no longer cared about. And you all know the rest of the story. Obviously, the point here is, don't judge a book by its cover.

## Metaphor Points of Construction

1. Change a client's personal reference to a character in the story.
    A. Audience = President
2. Pace the client's situation by linking behaviors and events be-tween the characters in the story and the client's situation.
    A. Audience = President
3. Find resources for the client within the context of the story.
    A. Audience's frame of mind = President's frame of mind

4. Make sure the story features events in which the characters in the story resolve the conflict and achieve the desired outcome.
    A. Don't judge a book by its cover.

**Pre-Steps**

1. Identify behavior and events
    A. Taking an appearance as the end decision
2. Strategy in question
    A. Look deeper
3. Desired outcomes
    A. Dig below the surface

**Mapping Strategies**

1. Displace referential characters.
    A. Establish characters (e.g., the president of Harvard, etc.)
    B. Preserve relationship
2. Establish a connection between the client's current situation or behavior and the characters' situations or behaviors.
3. Establish resources of the characters and events
    A. President =Small-minded
    B. Audience = Look deeper
4. Resolution
    A. Ambiguous
        i. Leave it the way the story reads now.
    B. Direct Connect
        i. Bring the story full circle to offers ways that the audience can look deeper into a client's situation.

# Scheduling Appointments and Setting Up Your Business

A few years ago, I turned 30. I never thought the day would come, but as I have gotten older my body has started to feel the toll.

My tumultuous medical history includes reconstructive shoulder surgery, a torn patella tendon, cartilage damage to my knee and severe tendonitis in my shoulder.

Once I turned 30, it really hit me that it was time to start treating my body right. So I found a place that specialized in physical therapy and chiropractic care called Peak Performance. The best thing about the place was their sales pitch.

They did everything right. Stories, metaphors, charts, graphs, asking for referrals, almost everything we've talked about up to this point. But what was most mind-boggling was the appointment process.

They wanted me to set up the next six months of appointments on the spot! I had plenty of excuses, but I couldn't beat their logic that it would be easier to schedule things now, while my calendar was still clear, then just cancel if I needed.

They said that I would experience greater value with a disciplined approach. Who could argue with that? I ended up committing to six months' worth of appointments right then and there. It's the same thing if you go to the dentist. I went last week, and they already have my next appointment set for six months from now.

We always say that we are like doctors, dentists or lawyers and thus we should prescribe to their scheduling methods. I have been in sales for over 10 years and have worked with three junior representatives during that time.

The biggest complaint I have heard from my peers is, "things are slow, if only I could fill my calendar."

Why not go to your top clients and tell it like this: "I see my top clients every six weeks [or whatever loop schedule you have], and I would like to be consistent with you.

What I would like to do is send you an Outlook scheduler and get X number of appointments scheduled with you.

Sure, you may need to reschedule if things get busy, but at least we are now committed to each other's business!" Now you have your top clients consistently on your calendar for the rest of the year.

**Metaphor Points of Construction**

1. Change a client's personal reference to a character in the story.
   A. Audience = My experience
2. Pace the client's situation by linking behaviors and events be-tween the characters in the story and the client's situation.
   A. Audience = My experience
3. Find resources for the client within the context of the story.
   A. Audience's techniques = Techniques in the story

4. Make sure the story features events in which the characters in the story resolve the conflict and achieve the desired outcome.
    A. Have a scheduling process

**Pre-Steps**

1. Identify behavior and events
    A. Not scheduling effectively
2. Strategy in question
    A. Scheduling
3. Desired outcomes
    A. Scheduling effectively and providing value

**Mapping Strategies**

1. Displace referential characters.
    A. Establish characters (e.g., me, etc.)
    B. Preserve relationship
2. Establish a connection between the client's current situation or behavior and the characters' situations or behaviors.
3. Establish resources of the characters and events
    A. Scheduling process
    B. Audience = Schedule more effectively
4. Resolution
    A. Ambiguous
        i. Leave it the way the story reads now.
    B. Direct Connect
        i. Bring the story full circle and describe ways that an audience can schedule more effectively.

## Green Eggs and Ham

I have been in sales for over 13 years. During that time, I have had many mentors help guide me along that path, teaching me a variety of skills and life lessons that have always led to some type of success.

Their methods have involved many different things to help me grow as an individual and as a business professional, and invariably, I have been recommended a huge number of books.

Over the past few years I have come across the most unlikely of mentors: my eight-year-old nephew, Tyler. A few years back, Tyler asked that I read him his favorite book, "Green Eggs and Ham," by Dr. Seuss.

"Green Eggs and Ham" was published in 1960 and continues to delight children everywhere, as it's the fourth best-selling children's hardcover book of all time.

But what you might not know is, this book is chock full of sales.

The book is about this short little Grinch guy who tries to get Sam-I-Am to eat Green Eggs and Ham. During the book, the Grinch asks Sam-I-Am to eat Green Eggs and Ham 13 times.

The Grinch is very persistent in asking Sam-I-Am to eat Green Eggs and Ham.

Of those 13 times, how many are different? The Grinch asks Sam-I-Am 13 different ways to eat Green Eggs and Ham.

Do you like Green Eggs and Ham?

Would you like them in a house?

Would you eat them in a box?

Would you like them here?

Would you?

Could you?

In a car?

Would you, could you, on a train?

Would you, could you, in the rain?

In the dark?

Would you, could you, in the dark?

You do not like Green Eggs and Ham?

Would you, could you, on a boat?

Finally, Sam-I-Am tries Green Eggs and Ham, and he exclaims, "I will eat them here and there. Say! I will eat them ANYWHERE!"

The story may be interpreted as a fable to encourage children to try new things. Perhaps fear, pride or a feeling of superiority are making the main character resistant to change and self-improvement.

This story can be used in various settings to hammer home the point of being persistent and creative.

**Metaphor Points of Construction**

1. Change a client's personal reference to a character in the story.
    A. Audience = Grinch
2. Pace the client's situation by linking behaviors and events be-tween the characters in the story and the client's situation.
    A. Audience = Grinch

3. Find resources for the client within the context of the story.
    A. Audience's techniques = Techniques in the story (persistent and creative)
4. Make sure the story features events in which the characters in the story resolve the conflict and achieve the desired outcome.
    A. Persistence and creativity

**Pre-Steps**

1. Identify behavior and events
    A. Persistence and creativity
2. Strategy in question
    A. Persistence and creativity
3. Desired outcomes
    A. More persistence and creativity

**Mapping Strategies**

1. Displace referential characters.
    A. Establish characters (e.g., the Grinch, etc.)
    B. Preserve relationship
2. Establish a connection between the client's current situation or behavior and the characters' situations or behaviors.
3. Establish resources of the characters and events.
    A. Persistent and creative behavior
    B. Audience = More persistent, creative behavior
4. Resolution
    A. Ambiguous
        i. Leave it the way the story reads now.
    B. Direct Connect

i. Bring the story full circle and detail ways that the audience can be more persistent and creative at what they do.

# Appendix: 3-D Communication

## Discover Your Preferred Representational System

*By Roger Ellerton, PhD, ISP, CMC, managing partner of Renewal Technologies, Inc.*

While the assessment is an important informational tool, the assessment is not fully definitive, as there are only 12 questions, and your preferred representational system may change over time or in different contexts.

In general, one representational system is not better than another. If you score low on one or more of the systems, you may wish to explore how this is affecting your life experiences.

Have fun with this assessment. I hope it provides you with additional insight on how you prefer to communicate with others.

### Instructions:

For each of the following statements, please assign a number to every phrase, using the following system:

**1 = Least descriptive of you**

**2 = Second least descriptive**

**3 = Second most descriptive**

**4 = Most descriptive**

If you have trouble deciding between two phrases, go with the first thought that comes to mind.

## Representational System Assessment



**1. When vacationing at the beach, the first thing that makes me glad to be there is:**

A.___ The feel of the cool sand, the warm sun or the fresh breeze on my face.

B.___ The roar of the waves, the whistling wind or the sound of birds in the distance.

C.___ This is the type of vacation that makes sense, or the cost is reasonable.

D.___ The scenery, the bright sun and the blue water.

**2. When overwhelmed, I find it helps if:**

A.___ I can see the big picture.

B.___ I can hear what's going on.

C.___ I can get in touch with what is happening.

D.___ I make sense of things in my head.

**3. When given an assignment at work, it is easier to carry out if:**

A.___ I can picture what is required.

B.___ I have a feel for what is required.

C.___ I have an understanding of what is required.

D.___ I have tuned into what's required.

**4. I find it easier to follow a presentation if:**

A.___ I feel in touch with the presenter and the material is within my grasp.

B.___ There is a visual display so that I can visualize the concepts.

C.___ The presentation is based on facts and figures and is logically presented.

D.___ The presenter speaks clearly with varying tonality or uses sound to emphasize the message.

**5. When buying a car, I make my decision based on:**

A.___ The purchase price, gas mileage, safety features, etc.

B.___ How comfortable the seats are, or the feeling I get when I test drive it.

C.___ The color, styling or how I would look in it.

D.___ The sound of the engine, or stereo system, or how quiet it rides.

**6. I communicate my thoughts through:**

A.___ The tone of my voice.

B.___ My words.

C.___ My appearance.

D.___ My feelings.

**7. When I am anxious, the first thing that happens is:**

A.___ Things begin to sound different.

B.___ Things begin to feel different.

C.___ Things begin to look different.

D.___ Things begin to make less sense.

**8. During a discussion, I am most often influenced by:**

A.___ The other person's logic.

B.___ The other person's tone of voice.

C.___ The energy I feel from the other person.

D.___ Seeing the other person's body language, or being able to picture the other person's viewpoint.

**9. I assess how well I am doing at work based on:**

A.___ My understanding of what needs to be done.

B.___ How I see myself making progress.

C.___ How things sound.

D.___ How satisfied I feel.

**10. One of my strengths is my ability to:**

A.___ See what needs to be done.

B.___ Make sense of new facts and data.

C.___ Hear what sounds right.

D.___ Get in touch with my feelings.

**11. I enjoy:**

A.___ Choosing a piece of music to listen to.

B.___ Making a logical, compelling point.

C.___ Choosing clothes that are comfortable.

D.___ Choosing clothes that look good.

**12. If you agree with someone, you are more likely to say:**

A.___ That feels right.

B.___ That looks right.

C.___ That sounds right.

D.___ That makes sense.

## Determining Your Preferences

1. Copy your answers to the lines below:

| Question | Visual | Auditory | Kinesthetic | Digital |
|---|---|---|---|---|
| 1 | D | B | A | C |
| 2 | A | B | C | D |
| 3 | A | D | B | C |
| 4 | B | D | A | C |
| 5 | C | D | B | A |
| 6 | C | A | D | B |
| 7 | C | A | B | D |
| 8 | D | B | C | A |
| 9 | B | C | D | A |
| 10 | A | C | D | B |
| 11 | D | A | C | B |
| 12 | B | C | A | D |
| Total | V = | A = | K = | D = |

2. Add the numbers in each column. A comparison of the totaled scores indicates your relative preference for each of the four major representational systems; the higher the score, the higher your preference.

The reason this knowledge is so powerful in not only sales and business, but all walks of life, is that we all communicate in our own preferred representational system. But our message is not as effective if it doesn't match the client's preferred representational system. We all want to eliminate the frustration of not being heard as we intend to be heard.

**Example Words**

The following are some words you can look for to help establish the preferred representational system of your customer.

| **Visual** | **Auditory** | **Kinesthetic** |
|---|---|---|
| Picture | Hear | Feel |
| Look | Listen | Touch |
| View | Sound | Grasp |
| Appear | Make music | Get a hold of |
| Show | Harmonize | Slip through |
| Dawn | Tune in/out | Catch on |
| Reveal | Be all ears | Tap into |
| Envision | Rings a bell | Make contact |
| Illuminate | Be heard | Turn around |
| Imagine | Silence | Throw out |
| Clear | Resonate | Hard |
| Foggy | Deaf | Unfeeling |
| Focused | Mellifluous | Concrete |
| Hazy | Dissonance | Scrape |
| Crystal | Question | Get a handle |
| Picture | Unhearing | Solid |

## Example Patterns of Speech

Next, you'll find speech patterns, styles and other communication tools that can offer additional clues as to a client's preferred representational system.

| | Visual/Auditory | Kinesthetic |
|---|---|---|
| Patterns of Speech | ☐ Fast talkers<br>• Filler words (um, uh, you know, etc.) | • Deliberate speech<br>• Wordy |
| Understanding | ☐ Quick<br>• Will change the subject | • Needs detail<br>• Needs to check in |
| Decision Process | ☐ Abstract to big picture<br>• Gambler | • Basic to detailed<br>• Speculative |
| Closing Statements | ☐ Ready to seize an opportunity | • Let's study and plan strategies |
| Excitement Level for Close | ☐ Fast and excited | ☐ Sincere and just |

## Example Phrases

Here, you'll find a selection of phrases commonly attributed to each style.

| **Visual** | Auditory | **Kinesthetic** |
|---|---|---|
| An eyeful | Afterthought | All washed up |
| Appears to me | Blabbermouth | Boils down to |
| Beyond a shadow of a doubt | Clear as a bell | Chip off the old block |
| Bird's eye view | Clearly expressed | Come to grips |
| Catch a glimpse | Call on | Control yourself |
| Clear-cut | Describe in detail | Cool/calm/collected |
| Dim view | Earful | Firm foundations |
| Flashed on | Give an account | Get a handle |
| Get a perspective on | Give me your ear | Get a load of this |
| Get a scope | Grant an audience | Get in touch with |
| Hazy idea | Heard voices | Get the drift |
| Horse of a different color | Hidden message | Get your goat |
| In light of | Hold your tongue | Hand in hand |
| In person | Idle talk | Hang in there |
| In view of | Inquire into | Heated argument |
| Looks like | Keynote speaker | Hold it |
| Make a scene | Loud and clear | Hold on |
| Mental image | Manner of speaking | Hothead |
| Mental picture | Pay attention to | Keep your shirt on |
| Mind's eye | Power of speech | Know-how |

| | | |
|---|---|---|
| Naked eye | Purrs like a kitten | Lay cards on the table |
| Paint a picture | State your purpose | Pain in the neck |
| See to it | Tattle-tale | Pull some strings |
| Short sighted | To tell the truth | Sharp as a tack |
| Showing off | Tongue-tied | Slipped my mind |
| Sight for sore eyes | Tuned in/tuned out | Smooth operator |
| Staring off into space | Unheard of | So-so |
| Take a peek | Utterly | Start from scratch |
| Tunnel vision | Voiced an opinion | Stiff upper lip |
| Under your nose | Well-informed | Stuffed shirt |
| Up front | Within hearing | Too much of a hassle |
| Well-defined | Word for word | Let me feel |
| Show me what you have | Tell me what you have | |

## Closing Statements

| **Visual** | **Auditory** | **Kinesthetic** |
|---|---|---|
| If this looks good in your mind's eye, we will go ahead and focus on getting in the paperwork. | If I could tell you a way you could... you would want to hear about it, right? | If I could help you get a grip of a solid way in which you could... you would want to get a feel for it, wouldn't you? |
| If I could show you an attractive way to... you would want to look at it, wouldn't you? | If it sounds good to you, we will discuss how to set up an account. | If this feels good to you, we will go ahead and set up an account by handling the paperwork. |

# About the Author: Matthew Linklater

MATT LINKLATER LIVES A PASSION FOR HELPING PEOPLE create financial freedom by giving them a roadmap for success.

He has over 15 years of experience meeting and interviewing over 13,000 financial advisors to bring to you a unique approach that you will not get from Wall Street or the media.

He prides himself on teaching families all over the world about money, how money works, and how to get money to work better for them.

Matt has written two books – Quick Witted and Counter Attack. He reached best-selling author status and became a member of National Academy of Best- Selling Authors for his work in Counter Attack.

He has also been featured in Inc. Magazine and on ABC, NBC, CBS, and Fox.

Matt is married to Denise Wayman. Matt and Denise enjoy working out, traveling, reading, and are on a constant quest for self-improvement. They are both Certified Personal Coaches in NLP and TLT™.

With all of the economic turmoil in the markets, the country and around the world, it's more vital than ever to keep your wealth safe and secure… but also growing.

Most importantly, Matt's mission is to help you protect your money from the Wall Street Casino, and build your wealth SAFELY and SECURELY.

Regardless of your financial situation Matt can help anyone get on the path to creating financial freedom and sleeping well at night.

33052747R00107

Made in the USA
Middletown, DE
28 June 2016